FROM A GREAT DREAM TO GRAND OPENING:

HOW TO START YOUR VERY OWN
Coffee Shop

STELLA PERRY

© 2019 From a Great Dream to Grand Opening: How to Start Your Very Own Coffee Shop.

All rights reserved. No part of the book may be reproduced in any shape or form without permission from the publisher.

This guide is written from a combination of experience and high-level research.

Even though we have done our best to ensure this book is accurate and up to date, there are no guarantees to the accuracy or completeness of the contents herein.

This cover has been designed using resources from Freepik.com

ISBN: 9781707610716

Reviews

Reviews and feedback help improve this book and the author. If you enjoy this book, we would greatly appreciate it if you could take a few moments to share your opinion and post a review on Amazon.

also by Stella Perry

Brewing and More. How to Enjoy Coffee Beyond Your Morning Routine

mybook.to/RoastingCoffee

Contents

Introduction	5
Step 1: Creating a Business Plan	9
What are you going to sell?	10
Where are you going to get it?	12
Who is your staff?	13
Who is your clientele?	14
What makes your business special?	15
Review local laws and health criteria	16
A Note About the Next Steps - A Brief Pep Talk	18
Step 2: Do the Math	19
What tools and resources will you need to help you?	19
How are you going to pay for it all?	23
Something Borrowed	24
Making New Friends and Investors	27
Step 3: Create the Space	29
Renting Vs. Buying	30
The Search for the Perfect Spot	32
Location Concerns	33
Finding the Perfect Price Point	34
Asking All the Right Questions	36
Making "Cents" of Your Space	37
Looking Out	39
Make Sure It's on the Up-And-Up	40
Step 4: Time to Go Shopping	42
Construction First	42
Go with the Flow	44
Define Your Style	45
The Big Supplies	47
Appliances Big and Small	49
An Important Reminder and a Second Pep Talk	50
Step 5: Bringing in the Product	51

Who You Serve Is What You Serve	51
A Snack to Suit the Crowd	52
Considering the Overall Menu	54
Sourcing Coffee	55
Creating Vs. Assembling Vs. Purchasing	56
On the Topic of Waste	60
Step 6: The Wild World of Marketing	**62**
Sign Here	63
Www. You're Going to Build a Website. Com	63
Follow Us On…	68
Important Things to Avoid on Social Media	71
The Method of Our Forefathers	72
All the Right Stuff	72
Step 7: The Hiring and Staffing Process	**75**
An Important Note about Labor Laws	75
Determine Who Does What … and When	76
Hire Carefully and Confidently	78
Learning All There is to Know	84
Be Demanding	86
Step 8: Planning for the Big Day	**88**
Setting the Stage	88
The Final Walkthrough	90
Planning Your Grand Opening	91
What Will Make Your Day Special?	92
Special Deals for a Special Day	94
What Do You Need When You Need a Helper?	95
Be Prepared	96
Business as Usual	**98**
Conclusion	**100**

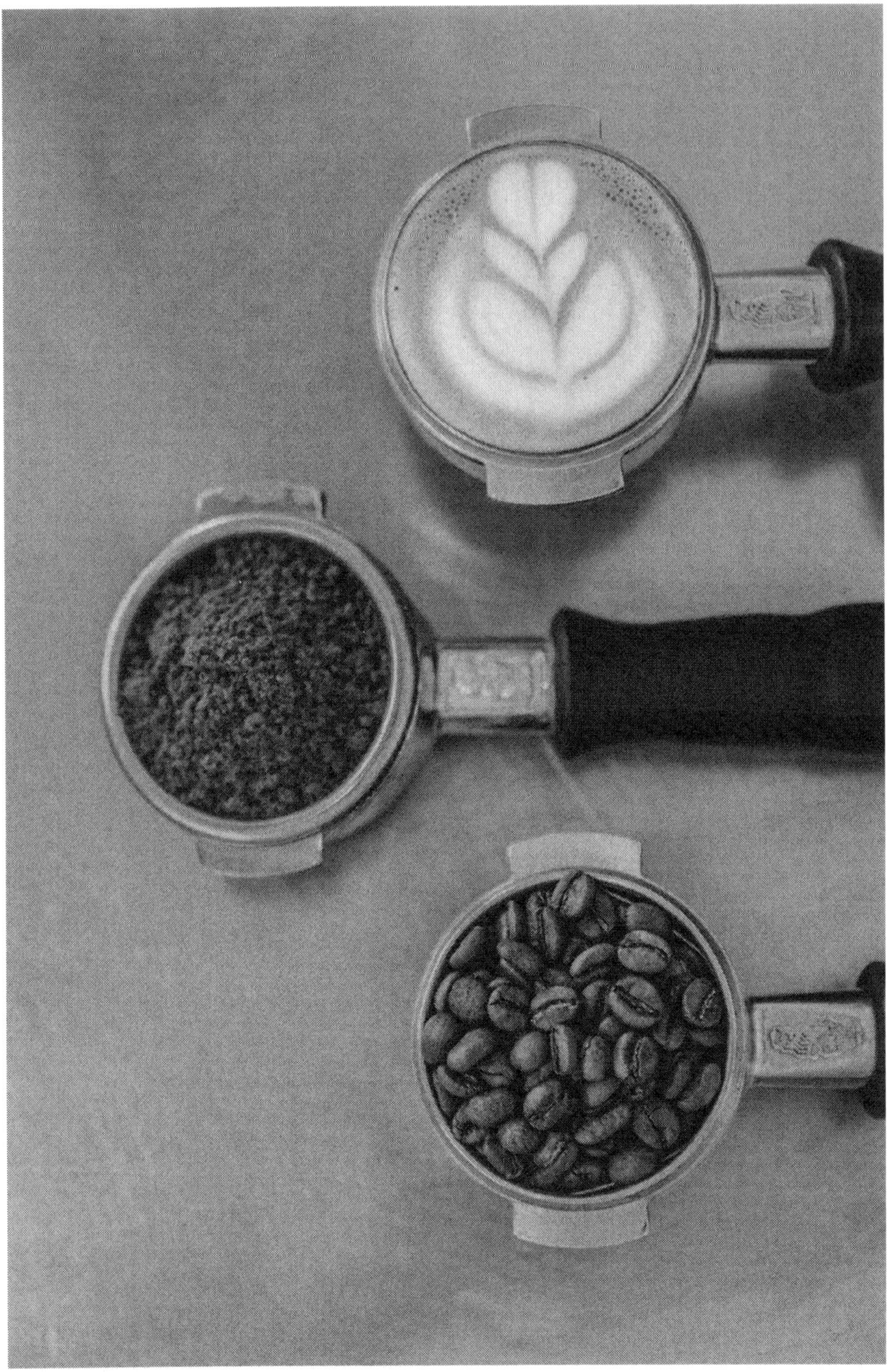

Introduction

There's something magical about a coffee shop. The warm, steamy aroma of roasted coffee beans and dripping espresso. The tasty treats that await inside glass cases. The shine of early morning light off the steel machinery. The bustling clink of ceramic mugs and plates that awakens the senses. That personal experience when the barista calls your name. And of course, that deep sense of satisfaction when the delicious beverage you've been craving is finally in your hand. Whether you're starting your day or grabbing an afternoon pick-me-up, very few of us take for granted the comfort of a friendly shop that has exactly what you want, exactly when you need it.

Many of us have very fond memories attached to coffee shops. Waiting out the rain with a steaming mug of a house blend. Working on a résumé for the hundredth time in search of the perfect job opportunity with a cup of tea bought with pocket change. Meeting with friends to catch up after far too long and giggling over lattes. That blind date with that one person who was actually worthy of a second date ... and lingering over an ambitiously large mocha. The first time you heard a local musician perform that song you love. The first time you stood up and read your poetry aloud to someone that wasn't your best friend. Coffee shops tend to be multi-functional places where we can revel in our thoughts, have meaningful social interactions, or just grab a cup of delicious caffeine on our way to our next destination in an overworked day.

Some of us are so deeply moved and inspired by these feelings and memories, we feel called to open our own coffee shop. It may seem a vague process at first. You purchase a good and worthy space, put some equipment in it, brew some coffee, and then there's a coffee shop, right? Well, those are all important steps, but the process of actually planning and opening a coffee shop requires a lot of thought, a lot of preparation, and an eye toward long-term success.

If you are willing to put in the hard work and dedicated to seeing every step all the way through, you will be able to open the doors to your coffee shop. All told, the process may take many months, or even years, as you accumulate all of the funding, fixtures, and furnishings for your coffee shop. We'll take a look at what to consider when trying to find the perfect location for your coffee shop, too. It is absolutely crucial that you are not in a rush to make things happen because some steps might take longer. There will be unexpected delays. There will be frustrations aplenty. You may be armed with a solid vision and a creative spirit, but you will also need a generous helping of patience and good humor.

You'll discover, as you wade deeper and deeper into this project, that you are surrounded by great resources. Many times in this book, we'll encourage you to do research. While you're likely already very well acquainted with Google and YouTube, you'll want to dive deeper. Talk to your friends and family. Network with people in the coffee shop or restaurant industry. This book combines knowledge from generations of individuals with experience in every aspect of running a business, from Human Resource experts, life-long baristas, franchisees, executive chefs, business owners, coffee fanatics, and commercial decorators. As you work toward your goal of opening your own coffee shop, you will wear all of these hats—sometimes it will feel like you're wearing them all at once! Stay focused and stay true to your vision and your budget. Stay calm, and your dreams will follow you anywhere!

There are many types of coffee shops, from drive-through roadside kiosks to grand cafe experiences. Some shops serve just one or two specialties, while others serve full menus of creative beverages and a rotating menu of seasonal sandwiches and meals. There are franchise coffee shops, independent mom-and-pop coffee shops, and coffee shops that operate within a mall or shop. This book is written to help guide you through many of the things any coffee shop owner will need to consider, but your specific location and situation may hold some slightly different or additional things to bear in mind. The number one recommendation of every professional in the food industry, regardless of capacity, is to always, *always* do your research.

There will be times when you need to consult a professional. Accountants, contractors, realtors, and lawyers are just a few of the resources you may need to add to your team as you move closer and closer to Opening Day. While it may be tempting to do as much work as possible on your own, think about how you would feel if your business began blossoming, only to be shut down due to an avoidable violation. When in doubt, paying a professional a bit now can save you endless expenses and frustration down the line when something goes wrong. This is not about opening a coffee shop as quickly and cheaply as you can; this is about arming yourself to make good decisions when creating your very own business.

As you read through this book, you'll notice we have included some helpful resources to get your imagination started. This includes some tables and charts you can incorporate into your own planning portfolio, as well as some links that can help guide you to various resources to get you started on your research. None of these should be considered exhaustive, but merely an illustration of the vast number of possibilities for your venture. We aren't specifically endorsing any particular method, supplier, or resource, but rather guiding you toward finding a solution that works best for your particular coffee shop, your budget, and your needs.

You may wish to take notes. You may wish to pause at a certain point to do a little internet searching. You may want to highlight concepts to think about later. Again, take your time with this process. Business owners know a lot, and savvy business owners never stop learning. From the very first concept of your business plan brainstorm session to cutting the ribbon at the grand opening, this book is designed to stimulate the thought process to make sure you are aware of the things many people never consider when first dreaming of opening their own coffee shop.

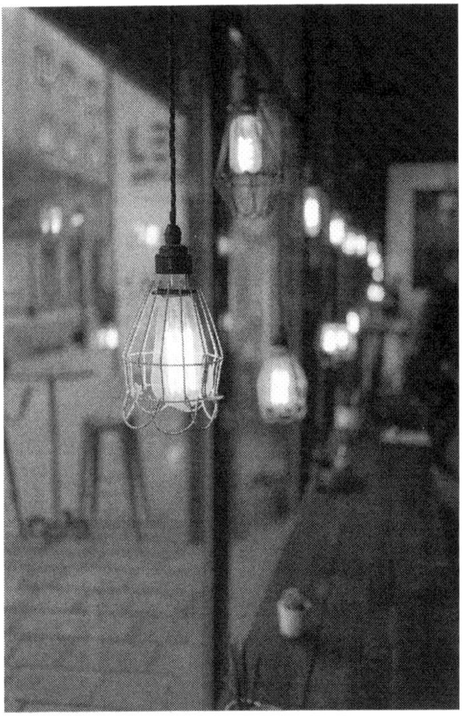

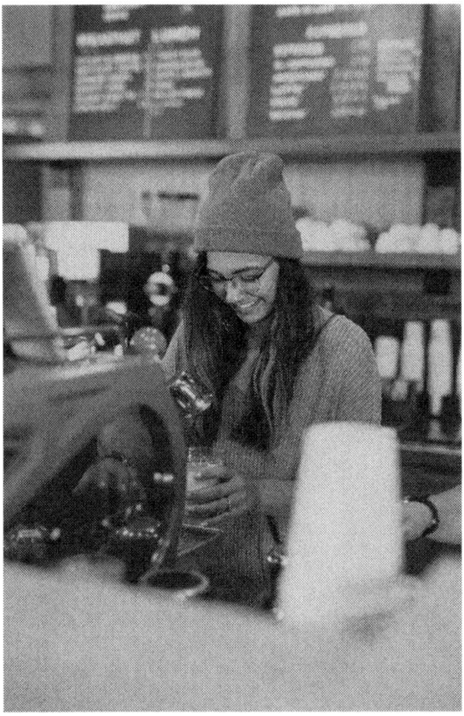

Step 1: Creating a Business Plan

There are two very important ingredients in any thriving business: a vision and a plan. For many of us, the vision comes first and that's a great place to start! By being aware of all the elements that need to go into both the vision and the plan, you can be well on your way toward making that dream come true. First, you need to iron out all of the details.

Brainstorming the business plan is a key step in realizing both the vision and the plan. You cannot skip or skimp on this step. In fact, you will likely revisit and revise this step many times—not only while working toward Opening Day, but throughout the life of your establishment. The business plan is all about forming the requirements that will make your business run successfully.

Research is key throughout the entire process, but especially in these early days of brainstorming. Whether you have a very solid vision of what you want your shop to look like or a vague idea of the flow of things, you'll need to invest some time and thought into creating the business plan. There are quite a few things you'll need to do before you even get started.

Visit as many coffee shops as you can. Big chains. Little independent shops. Bakeries that happen to sell coffee. If there's a shop in your niche, pop in. Grab a cup of coffee and observe what makes the place run. Who is the clientele? Do they seem to be regulars, or just passing through? How many people are on staff? How does the coffee taste? What is the mood of the place? As you visit more and more shops, you'll see how different aspects make different shops tick, and as you observe these varying methods and environments, you may start picking out things you'd like to add to your plan, and things you definitely don't want in your shop.

As you're in this brainstorming stage, it's a good idea to have a notepad or tablet with you at all times. Inspiration can come anywhere and anytime. No detail is insignificant at this point, even if they conflict with each other. Your goal is to create a thriving business that reflects you and your imagination. Remember, you're going to be responsible for every single detail of this business, from the color of the cups to the volume of the ambient music.

The more thoughts you capture now, the easier it will be to whittle them down into a business plan. Eventually, as you do more and more research, these seemingly scattered thoughts and notes will start becoming cohesive. You'll start thinking in terms of "how will I do that in my shop?" You'll watch servers create frothy concoctions and wonder if your future employee will be able to match their performance. Every experience you have in a coffee shop from now on is going to be a learning experience. You may never look at a cup of coffee the same way again!

What are you going to sell?

The key ingredient of a coffee shop is, of course, coffee. But what kind of coffee? There are so many options out there. Flavored, internationally sourced, locally roasted, espresso, decaffeinated ... there are far more options these days than "regular or decaf."

Are you going to serve specialty drinks? If so, what kinds? While what you brainstorm now doesn't have to be fully committed to the menu, get a feel for what you'd like to serve. More importantly, consider how you'll serve it. For example, if you'd like to offer a mocha beverage, write out the ingredients: espresso, milk, and chocolate. What types of milk would you like to offer your customers? How about temperature? Some coffee shops offer the choice of a hot mocha, an iced mocha, or a frozen mocha. Offering these options requires the same ingredients, but also ice, a blender, and different cup options. Later, we're going to get more involved in the concept of inventory and sourcing, but none of that can be done until you have an idea of what is going to go into those cups.

Speaking of cups, what sizes will the beverages be? Not only will hot and cold drinks require different types of cups, but offering different sizes will require different stock as well. Will beverages be served differently if they are "for here" or "to go"? What about straws? Plastic straws tend to be an environmental concern, but paper straws can dissolve, and stainless steel straws can be expensive. Again, this is not the time to dive into the budget concerns—that will come soon enough—but now is when you consider the overall logistics of what goes where and how.

Once you've got a feel for how the "coffee" part of the coffee shop will look, what about non-coffee drinks? Will you offer hot tea, and if so, what kinds? What about kids' drinks, like hot chocolate or juice? What about ice water?

How about food? Will you make your own food? Will you have bakers or sandwich makers on staff, or will you bring in food from a local bakery or sandwich shop? Food can be extra tricky, because you need to consider peak times at your coffee shop, and what kind of appetite your clientele may have. At this stage, it's best to jot down a few ideas of foods and treats you would like to serve, then revisit this as plans become more clear. We'll get much more in-depth about the food process, but at this stage, you'll want to have some general ideas about your overall goals for serving tasty treats to your customers.

Try to dream up scenarios in which customers come to your coffee shop, so you can walk through what they may want. Let's say customers come into your shop on their way to work. They might want a hand-held, easy-to-eat sandwich or pastry to take with them. On the other hand, students that come to study in your space might want a snack to enjoy while they read or write. Moms stopping by for a pick-me-up while shuttling the kids from school to activities might want to grab quick snacks for the kids, as well.

Select a few options for each type of situation. For example:

Breakfast: cinnamon rolls, apple danish, bran muffins, chocolate chip muffins, bear claws
Sandwiches to go: egg and cheese, bagel and cream cheese, sausage, egg, and cheese
In-house breakfast: egg and sausage with toast, breakfast potatoes
Cookies: peanut butter, chocolate chip, frosted sugar
Snacks: crispy rice treats, granola, fresh fruit, cheese and crackers

This is not meant to be an all-inclusive list, but simply an example of some of the situations in which patrons of your coffee shop may want to grab a bite to eat in addition to their beverage. Again, the goal of this exercise is to set the parameters and bring the vision further into focus. You may ultimately scrap every menu decision you make here, but this is a great start to forming your ideas. By considering who you hope your patrons to be, you can anticipate how you can best capture their needs with your business plan, which will lead you closer to your goal of opening your coffee shop.

Where are you going to get it?

Sourcing your beverages and food items is a crucial step that can help you understand what is feasible for your business model. We'll drill down into this topic in a future chapter, but this is a good time to brainstorm places where you can get the products you want.

For example, if you really love the cinnamon rolls at the bakery down the street, you have the option to see if the bakery would be willing to work with you to supply their rolls, or you can start
searching for a recipe that accurately mimics their product. Each option

comes with its own considerations. If you're going to contract with a bakery to supply their goods, you'll have to be able to get a feel for supply and demand so you can order the correct inventory. If you're going to make them yourself, you'll have to consider purchasing all of the ingredients and having a space to make a large volume of cinnamon rolls. If that space is off-site, you'll also have to consider transporting those rolls to the coffee shop and storing them.

For each of the items you've considered serving, jot down some places where you can get what's needed to make that item. Consider local wholesale shops or stores that offer wholesale discounts. What about national suppliers? Don't worry about comparing costs at this point—this is the part of the process where you let the ideas flow. Include every possible avenue so you can have the most possible options at your fingertips.

Who is your staff?

As you consider what you're going to serve, you'll need to consider how it's going to be served. Beyond "in a cup" or "on a plate," consider how your coffee shop will be run. What roles will each staff member have?

You might want to map out the flow of how an order might be processed. For example:

Customer orders at register > cashier rings up the order and gives order to barista > barista makes and serves the drink > food is managed by a third staff member, who plates or bags the food items and hands them to the customer

Or

Customer orders at register > barista both rings up the order and begins to make the drink and food > once all food and beverages are complete, they are handed back to the customer

Each process has its pros and cons and may be more feasible at different times of the day. During peak time, having one staff member handle all of the steps might create a lag in taking and processing new orders. At the same time, this might be the perfect process during slower times of the day. To determine the best fit, you need to figure out who will be in your coffee shop, and when.

Who is your clientele?

Nearly everyone can find something to love about a coffee shop, so it's always a good idea to be warm and welcoming to anyone who might be seeking a hot beverage and a treat. At the same time, you might be interested in creating a footprint in a particular niche.

If you live in a town with a large college or university, you might be interested in catering to the students and faculty. You might consider offering student discounts and free Wi-Fi. If you want to create a welcoming place for students to work, you'll want to consider things like low-volume music, electrical outlets for laptops and other device chargers, ambient lighting for reading, and seats that are comfortable. You may also consider that a student will take up space for a longer period of time but may make fewer purchases during that time since they are focused more on their work than ordering large amounts of food and drink.

Perhaps you want to create a meeting space. In that case, you might want to offer larger tables that accommodate gatherings of people, or spaces that are more private, so these groups do not interfere with other patrons. You might want to offer share-size snacks for these groups or carafes of coffee that can be enjoyed while they meet and discuss business.

If you'd like to build a child-friendly coffee shop, you might consider having some books or activities like coloring books on hand. You can even create small "busy bags" that can be checked out from the counter that keep younger minds and hands entertained while parents take a moment out of their busy day for a comforting beverage and a little peace and quiet. You'll also want to have food and drink that are suitable for kids, like non-caffeinated beverages, and food that doesn't create a giant mess that staff will have to clean up.

Traditionally, creative types flock to coffee shops. Will you offer exhibits for local artists? Open mic night for poets, writers, singers, and musicians? Will you have live music from time to time? All of these special events can be a great draw for customers but will require additional equipment, appropriate space, and considerations for supplies and staffing. Knowing what you want to happen in your space will help you narrow down your business plan to accommodate these interesting points.

What makes your business special?

Hand-in-hand with considering clientele is deciding why customers will want to come to your coffee shop. What sets you apart from the chain shops that can be found on nearly every corner? What will make a customer prefer to stop at your shop, rather than heading through the drive-thru of a local franchise?

For many people, the environment of a coffee shop is key. Is it bright and bustling, or dim and offers privacy? Are the drinks creative and flavorful? Do you showcase local artists, musicians, and more? For some, just having super-comfortable chairs can be a huge draw, especially for students who might miss the comforts of home. Anything you do to set your coffee shop apart from any other shop is the niche that you will fill, so consider all of the research you've done. What do regulars want? What do regulars LOVE? What types of things will make people want to come to your coffee shop before any other coffee shop?

Let your own tastes and personality shine here. The more you love your concept, the more you'll be devoted to watching it flourish. If you only half-heartedly appreciate your concept, you might devote less time to making it work. There are plenty of ways you can let your own interests shine in your coffee shop without going overboard. If you love books, consider having a wall of books patrons can read while they enjoy their drinks. This will put you on the hunt for unique books to add to your collection. If you enjoy plants, perhaps your coffee shop includes a beautiful array of succulents and indoor plants that give the environment a clean, homey feel. If you are a music enthusiast, perhaps you can cultivate an amazing collection of records to play so your patrons can discover a new favorite.

These are, of course, just a few ideas as to how your coffee shop can become unique and attract clientele. This is an opportunity to express your passions, so think of things that you share and enjoy with others, then think of fun ways to share that passion with even more and more people. Be creative and jot down a few possibilities!

Review local laws and health criteria

As full disclosure, please note that this book was written with the United States market in mind, so for those outside the US, please take the time to look up both local and federal laws for your area. Compliance with laws and health codes is absolutely crucial when it comes to running a business that involves serving food and drink. In many places, health code scores are posted publicly, and a poor mark or negative review can absolutely ruin a business at any time.

When considering your concept, do research on what is and isn't acceptable due to law and health code. For example, cat cafes (and even more exotic animal-themed cafes!) are popping up everywhere, but have a very distinct code as to how animals can come in contact with the customers, and frequently require waivers for patrons who may become inadvertently harmed by the animals.

Health codes vary from state to state and can change, depending on whether food is served in-house or if you choose not to serve food at all. There are codes for sanitation, codes for storing food, codes for cleanliness, and more. Be aware of all the restrictions and regulations before committing to a concept! There are far too many rules and regulations to list here, but some helpful links to get you started have been included in the index.

At this stage, you may have tons and tons of notes regarding your own coffee shop, and if you're a bit bewildered, you've done it right. Now is the time to slowly narrow things down a bit until you have a solid concept. This may not be accomplished in one day. You may find yourself running idea after idea past a trusted friend or family member. You may wish to spread all of your notes out on a large surface and piece them together one by one like a giant puzzle, or you may want to create a digital work board of how things will work. Some people even prefer to draw out their ideas to have a visual of how things will flow. Whatever your preferred method is, be sure to have all of your digital files clearly labeled, and all of your physical documents neatly stored. This process is going to be chaotic enough without trying to find that one specific note that you thought you put here, over and over again.

Take your time at this point. Don't rush ahead to get started without knowing exactly what you're looking to start. Really research drink recipes—we've included a few examples in the index to get the creative java juices flowing—and consider what you want to serve. Dive deep into your community to figure out who your customers are going to be, as well as what kind of space will best serve them. And most importantly, create a plan that you can feel committed to and passionate about, and ready to invest in fully.

A Note About the Next Steps – A Brief Pep Talk

Your business plan has now officially begun, but you're far from done at this point. In this first step, you have created the master plan upon which all of the next steps will rely. As you proceed, your plan will very likely change. Be flexible. Keep a focus on what you really want to accomplish with your coffee shop, but acknowledge that reality is what it is. You will encounter many setbacks along the way, and sometimes it will feel as if things are "too easy." The reason we establish these plans so early in the process is because they can always be revisited and changed.

Before you continue, really stop and think about how you're going to define success. Will you be happy when you open the doors on any old coffee shop, or will you not rest until the marble countertops match the swatch you've saved for years? There's no wrong answer here, but compromise is very, very important when building your business. As we proceed, you'll establish an overall budget, you'll find the right location, and we'll go shopping for all of the items you need to open your very own coffee shop. Start with big dreams, but be careful that you don't get swept away with extravagances, or start too small to sustain your business. Regardless of where your vision and plan start and end, the ultimate goal is to create a profitable business that reflects your ideal coffee shop.

Step 2: Do the Math

In the first step, we carefully created a business plan by jotting down all of the ideas and thoughts and considerations for your future business and carefully considering all your ideas into a plan that just might work. You have taken the time to do research and learned what makes similar businesses in your area thrive. By brainstorming every possible detail, you have taken the opportunity to consider a lot of options before settling on the one that speaks most to your vision and plan.

The goal of the first step was to create the overall blueprint to follow as you strive toward the grand opening of your very own coffee shop, but it's important that you do not discard all of your notes just yet! In this step, we'll be putting together the financial considerations of your new enterprise. Bear in mind that this step is about finding out what you can afford, and how to afford it. As the numbers tally up, you may find that some dreams are a bit out of your budget for now and having alternative options at hand can be helpful to keep you pressing forward toward fulfilling your dreams, rather than reaching a stalling point.

What tools and resources will you need to help you?

For many new business owners, this is a good time to consider hiring an accountant. While coming up with the figures you can afford is something you may feel comfortable doing yourself, a professional can help you take into consideration any taxes or fees that might be required in your area. A professional accountant can also help you organize all of your receipts, paperwork, and deeds to ensure you're prepared for every financial consideration, too.

Depending on your own abilities with keeping track of expenses and income, you may feel comfortable consulting with the accountant at the start of business and come tax time. There are many software options that are also available for business owners, and once you are set straight on the path of keeping records with professional help, you may be perfectly comfortable sorting all these records yourself. We've included a few examples of these types of software in the index, but ask yourself these important questions when choosing an option that fits your comfort level and business:

1. How comfortable are you with bookkeeping? Be honest with yourself. While the software will do the math for you, it will only be as good as the person entering figures. Take into consideration your financial literacy to ensure that the software you choose is something you can comfortably work with every single day.

2. Do plenty of research. There are specific types of software for small cafes and shops that might suit your anticipated business needs. Take a look at what features each option offers. Do you need a cloud-based program, which you can operate from any computer or device, anywhere? Do you need a program that offers 24-hour support? Do you want your bookkeeping software to include payroll functionality?

3. What about budget? Most software programs have a monthly cost associated with them, so when considering your monthly expenses, don't forget to include your bookkeeping software!

4. Data security considerations must be addressed, as well. How does this particular software back up and provide security for the data that you enter?

Keeping each of these questions in mind will help you as you discover and analyze the different types of bookkeeping software available to you. Be sure to be honest with yourself at every step—while it may seem easy to keep track of taxes for a small workforce, what happens when your staff grows? What if the taxation regulations change in your area? Will you be able to teach another partner how to use this software, in the event that you need to step away for a day off? Discuss these concerns with your accountant, if you're unsure of how to answer these questions on your own.

Now, let's consider the actual expenses that would be associated with the actual start-up of your coffee shop. Your goal will be to create a table that outlines each expense as a line item. This will not only help you stay organized for your own benefit, but many financiers require detailed business plans with these figures, as well. At this point, though, the goal is to get a general idea of what you might need. Instead of line items, you might have general categories at this point. For now, leave the "cost" section blank. Take this process step-by-step so you can truly consider where you want—and need—your hard-earned money to go to create the best profit. You'll revisit this table many times as we walk through all the considerations of opening your coffee shop. Line items may change over time, and you might be surprised by some of the dollar amounts you enter in the cost section, but creating a simple chart like this will help you stay organized and aware of your budget at all times.

Your first version of this table might look a bit like this. As you get closer and closer to Opening Day, you'll move further away from estimating the cost per category of expenses, and have an actual to-the-penny figure for individual line items. Remember: this is a process that starts big and becomes more and more refined as you get closer to your goal.

First Month's Lease and Security Deposit/ Down Payment and Mortgage

Insurance

Inspection Fees (health inspection, OSHA, HVAC, etc) and Code Prep

Utility Connection Fees and Deposits (water, electric, gas, trash removal, recycling, etc)

Business License and Legal

Office equipment: Register, POS system, receipt printer, order ticket printer (if necessary), credit card reader, printer paper, pens/notebooks, computer for bookkeeping

Coffee Equipment: Espresso Machine, Coffee Makers, Coffee Pots, Carafes, Bean Grinders, Espresso Cups and Filters, Milk Pitchers, Hot Water Steaming Equipment, Thermometers

Other Appliances: Oven, Refrigerator, Freezer, Icemaker, Cold Case, Display Case, Toaster, Microwave, Blenders, Prep Sinks, Dishwasher, Bathroom Equipment (if not included in the space)

Serving Equipment: Cups, Saucers, Plates, Utensils, Tongs, Spatulas

Paper Goods: Wrappers, Napkins, To Go Cups (hot and cold), Lids (hot and cold), Stir Sticks, Cup Sleeves, Straws, Toilet Paper, Paper Towels

Cleaning Supplies: Disinfectant per local procedure for all dishes, surfaces, restrooms, tables, floors, etc., Mops, Buckets, Brooms, Dustpans, Cloths for cleaning spills, Supplies for keeping windows clean

Uniforms for staff

Furniture: Chairs, tables, service counters, counters on which to place machinery, trash bins, storage and shelving

Labor/Staffing

Product: Coffee, syrups, milk, all per the recipes you finalize

Decor: painting the walls, finishing the floor, light fixtures, sound system, security system (if not supplied by space)

This list is, of course, just an example of some of the things you may or may not need to open your own coffee shop. Modify your chart for your own business; for example, if you do not plan to serve any type of food, you will not need things like a toaster, an oven, or plates. You may choose not to have a display case or cold case for grab-and-go items. Regardless of the items that actually fill your list, make sure you've considered every aspect of daily business. This list will be your guide for each following step of the process, from finding a location and space to fit your needs to determining supply chain, to shopping for the bits and pieces that bring your business's ambiance to life.

How are you going to pay for it all?

Now that you have an idea of what you're going to need to bring this dream to life, it's time to consider where the money is going to come from. You may have your own savings to put toward start-up, but as you dive into the details, you may start to realize that perhaps a little bit more is needed to provide ample padding for all of the "what ifs" that you most assuredly will encounter.

Let's start with your own savings. What do you have in your own bank account? Keep in mind, the world will not stand still while you focus on opening your coffee shop. You'll still need to pay your monthly bills, so set aside your active budget and don't touch it. Getting financing down the line on any rental space, equipment, and more will be deeply impaired if you default on any of your existing expenses. Keep your own financial record as clean as possible to ensure you have the capacity and options available for any financial assistance you may need throughout the process.

Putting aside the funds that you will need for your personal expenses, as well as a buffer for your own emergency needs, consider what part of your overall savings you're willing to commit to your new business. The temptation to cash out all of your retirement funds or investments may be high, but keep in mind that doing so may have tax implications, as well as depleting your nest egg. This is another part of the process in which having a professional accountant on hand will help mitigate any accidental financial mishaps you may make without realizing it!

Next, consider what you want to have in hand as start-up capital. While we haven't assigned prices to all of the items you'll need in order to open your doors, consider how much you can feasibly have available before you get started.

Something Borrowed

One option is to pursue a loan. There are many, many loans available for small business owners, so it is absolutely essential to do a considerable amount of research here. Your bank or financial institution may have loan options available. The Small Business Association is another potential source for a loan, as well. Companies like Swift Capital specialize in fast, online loans for small business owners.

As you do your research, you'll see a lot of unfamiliar terms that may make your head swirl. Since you're going into this venture as a new business owner, you're going to need to choose a loan program that makes sense while you wait to collect on profit. In addition to your regular expenses, and the expenses of running a business, you will need to pay the loan back as well, so be careful when reading all of the terms and conditions. You may be interested in one or more of the following options:

- A small business line of credit, which will provide a certain amount of funds, upon which you can draw credit with a monthly interest rate.
- Working capital loans can be very short-term loans to help a business owner have the funds on hand to deal with day-to-day expenses in times where profit can be uncertain.
- Term loans are a frequently chosen option for start-ups, as they come with a set dollar amount, and generally a fixed interest rate.
- Equipment loans are, as the name suggests, strictly for the purchase of equipment, and typically require a 20% down payment. These are generally secured through an equipment vendor, but may be sought elsewhere.
- Small business credit cards. Like the credit card you may carry in your wallet each day, there are both pros and cons of pursuing this option. You'll be able to easily track business expenses by applying them to this card alone, but interest rates could get out of hand if payments aren't made promptly and in full.

Another option for pursuing funding is to engage a partner or a group of investors. These are people, groups, and services that are willing to provide funding either with or without a cost to you. Some of these may seem too good to be true, in which case they probably are. There are still many reputable lending programs that can aid you in start-up capital for your coffee shop.

- Online lending platforms: Prosper, TrustLeaf, OnDeck, and Lending Club.
- Personal marketing: You may have friends or family members who are willing to gift you some cash to get started. There may be others in your circle who are willing to join you in your venture. Some people say it's best to avoid doing business with friends and family; however, there are generations of family-run businesses that say otherwise. Only you will be able to evaluate the relationship you have with potential investors within your circle, and how much control they wish to exercise over your business.
- Incubators and accelerators: These businesses help make your dreams of owning a business a reality. Not only do these groups offer potential investors, but also mentors, networking opportunities, and solid expertise. The National Business Incubation Association offers a directory of options that can help you find resources in your state, as well as local economic development services, and locations of Small Business Association resources in your area.
- Angel Networks: Angel Networks seem heaven-sent. These groups provide investors who can provide guidance and mentorship through the early processes of starting your business. This is a fantastic way to connect those who wish to inspire future business leaders in your niche with those, like you, who are wading into the unfamiliar waters of starting your very first enterprise.

Making New Friends and Investors

Another option, which is very popular in this social day and age, is crowdfunding. There are several websites that allow you to request funds from interested parties, such as Kickstarter, Peerbackers, OurCrowd, and Indiegogo. Each site has its own typical audience, and your intention to raise funds for your coffee shop can be broadcast in various ways, such as email, newsletter, and social media. Social media is, of course, an excellent choice for spreading the word, as each person who sees the post has the option of sharing the post with others. While crowdfunding typically raises donations in smaller amounts, it often garners a great deal of attention, helping you market your brand and bring your coffee shop into the limelight before the doors even open!

One source of crowdfunding that can be lots of fun is the old-fashioned method of getting out in the public. Announce your intentions to the community. Participate in community events on behalf of your business. For example, if your community has a flea market or craft event, team up with vendors to raise funds toward the opening of your shop. In fact, if you're handy, or have friends willing to donate to the cause, you could become a vendor yourself! Show up on behalf of your brand at places where the community gathers, be it street fairs, art fairs, or cultural events, and get the local folks excited about the new business that will soon be on their doorsteps. You may need to print some logo items or have samples available, but that level of investment will be small, compared to the potential funds that could head your way from excited investors and future customers. In fact, if you plan to provide space for local groups to meet, artists to exhibit, or musicians to perform, this is a great place to start networking with them.

At this stage, you've got some rudimentary plans for gaining the funding you need to proceed with the next steps. Often, you'll need to have a very solid business plan in place before applying for a loan of any kind, so the steps going forward from here will often lead back to the first step of creating a business plan, and this step of gaining the financial security to start shopping. Planning a business of any kind tends to be less linear and more circular, but if you start investigating financial options now, you'll have a better idea of your actual budget as you proceed with finding your shop and filling it with everything you'll need to make your coffee shop a success.

Step 3: Create the Space

Having a solid business plan is a requirement, and having a budget is crucial, but there's one really important element that will help bring this whole dream together: a space!

Many people want to choose the space before the first two steps, but there are a few important reasons to resist this urge. First, you need to know what the overall business will look like in order to know what type of space you need. This is why we drew up the business plan first. Perhaps, after looking at all your ideas and dreams, you discovered that a kiosk type of space would be absolutely perfect for your coffee shop. Alternately, you might realize you want to open a bakery in conjunction with your coffee shop, which requires space (and budget) for ovens and serving. In working with potential investors and mentors, perhaps you realized a few things about the capacity of your start-up, or in working within the community, you learned that there was an appetite amongst your peers for a totally different type of space than you initially envisioned.

As the pieces of the puzzle come together, you may find yourself revisiting and revamping your business plan over and over. The final business plan, which you may submit to receive financial backing, may look very different from your original daydreams, and while that may seem frustrating, it's generally a good thing. Your final business plan should reflect an operation that can financially sustain itself and bring benefits to the community. Success should not be measured by whether you get the perfect wall sconces, but whether your coffee shop is appreciated by its customers and brings in a profit over time. Keep this in mind as you start looking for the perfect spot for your coffee shop.

Renting Vs. Buying

Your very first consideration should be whether you wish to buy your location or lease. There are, of course, pros and cons to each decision. If you don't have the capital to purchase the location, then this option is off the table immediately, and leasing wins this round, but there are some things to keep in mind when considering each option.

When leasing, it needs to be clearly established what the property owner does and does not permit, as far as any upgrades or remodelling of the property. If the property owner won't let you make the adjustments that might be required to bring the property up to code, it won't work out. This is why we took the time to research laws and regulations when creating a business plan. You should be largely aware of what is required to make your business legal, and discuss these needs with the property owner before settling into a contract.

It's also very important that both the landlord and you agree on who is responsible for what. This can include everything from maintenance issues (what happens if the HVAC system quits and the business has to close for a few days?) to repair of the property (who makes sure the parking lot is paved?), to liability issues (who is considered liable if a tree falls on a customer's car during a wind storm?), to seasonal maintenance (who is responsible for snow removal?). A lot of these issues boil down to insurance agreements, which we'll discuss shortly, but very frequently, a landlord may cover these types of issues in the rental agreement, especially in the case of areas that may be shared between several businesses, like parking lots or HVAC systems.

You also need to examine the terms of the lease. What happens if the business does not succeed? We're obviously working toward putting our best foot forward and gaining profit, but unexpected things can happen that are far, far out of our control. What happens to the lease if you have to abruptly pull the plug on the coffee shop at any time? What happens to the contents of the building—do you have a set amount of time to remove your property? How much notice does the landlord require? It is generally in the landlord's best interest to have that spot occupied, so there may be an escape clause of sorts, but you might be charged a fee. It is always best to know these things ahead of time to avoid unpleasant surprises or visits from debt collectors.

What about buying? Generally speaking, buying a spot isn't within the budget or project scope for a first-time entrepreneur, but there are always exceptions to every rule. If you have experience with property management, buying a space might be a long-term investment that goes beyond this coffee shop plan. Business may go incredibly well, and you'll wish to expand in a few years, in which case you can lease out the original space to new tenants.

As the owner, you control everything. You can create your dream property, whether through remodeling or building from the ground up. You can control every inch of electric wiring, every screw and nail, and every inch of paint. Yes, that is going to require more money. Yes, that is going to require more time. However, having this level of control means your rent will never change. You will never have to argue with the property owner over who should take care of what. Furthermore, you can manage this property for the rest of your life.

At the same time, owning the space means you are responsible for absolutely everything. Every expense. Every insurance claim. Every legal requirement. Every zoning consideration. Just like with a house, any time anything goes wrong, it is automatically your responsibility. Are you prepared for that level of financial commitment?

The Search for the Perfect Spot

Once you've decided whether to lease or buy your space, you'll be able to start the search. You've probably begun a few preliminary internet searches for the perfect space for your coffee shop. It's always a good idea to look and to keep looking. While you may feel pressured to take the first space that might "kinda sorta" work, it is very important to remember that this shop is going to be your investment, and it won't work just because you want it to work. Having many options to review will help you understand what criteria you really need to make your business plan work. You may feel that having a lot of options will cloud your judgment or make the selection process more difficult, but consider each option a learning experience.

When you enter "coffee shop for sale" or "coffee shop for rent" in Google, you'll probably find thousands of results, some of which may not be entirely relevant. You may want to be more specific, such as "coffee shop for sale in TOWN" or "restaurant space for rent in TOWN." You may want the assistance of a professional and look for a "commercial real estate agent in TOWN," in order to find agents who assist people like you in finding their perfect space.

Each day, try a different type of search and make note of the results. There will be some spaces that very obviously will not work, and you can dismiss those right away. The rest of the spaces will likely fall under three categories: Maybe, Good Fit, and Dream. "Maybes" will be spaces that don't immediately make your heart flutter, but that check off most of the things you need for your coffee shop to open. "Good Fits" will be in the right price range, the right location, and have generally what you need to get started. "Dream" spaces will be those that maybe you can't afford right now, or might be bigger than what you need, or might require some additional permits that you're not sure you have the patience for right now, but would otherwise be ideal.

Location Concerns

For each space that makes it to the Maybe, Good Fit, and Dream list, conduct a drive-by. In fact, conduct a drive-by, park, and walk up. Finding a space for your coffee shop isn't just about finding the prettiest storefront. As anyone with real estate experience will tell you, the most important thing is LOCATION, LOCATION, LOCATION!

Your coffee shop has to allow people to visit it. That means that the location has to be convenient for your customers. If customers have to take several one-way streets to find your shop in an alley, it is highly unlikely they'll want to detour from their daily commute just for a quick cup of coffee. At the same time, if your shop is located on an extremely busy roadway with considerable traffic, customers may be anxious to just get through all the congestion and get to work already, making them less likely to stop. Additionally, your coffee shop should be easy to find from the road. The signage and entrance should be obvious enough that even morning, bleary-eyed, pre-caffeinated drivers can easily spot it and turn in.

Once they've arrived, customers need to be able to approach the building. It may seem obvious, but consider who your clientele will be, and where they'll be coming from, as decided in your business plan. Does this space have access to abundant parking? Can local customers walk to this space? Where will the deliveries of products and supplies be made? If you plan to host events, where will people be able to unload? All of these functions must allow for the flow of traffic on the street, and not block a shared parking lot if one exists. Customers should be able to enter, park, and leave easily without becoming frustrated or having a traffic mishap. If you plan to have a drive-thru window, the flow of this traffic needs to be considered, as well.

Accessibility is another concern. The Americans with Disability Act has a variety of requirements for restaurants and coffee shops, which were part of the legal review in Step 1. Not only do these requirements impact the inside of the coffee shop, but the parking lot and entrance, as well. If you are leasing a property, this may be something the property owner has already considered, but it's always good to make sure the entire facility is compliant before you get into a situation that could negatively impact your business!

Finding the Perfect Price Point

In Step 2, we started budget considerations and outlined all of the things that will be needed before the doors open. You may have hired an accountant to help you with all of the ins and outs along the way. You may have secured—or are in the process of securing—loans for your business. This is the stage where you need to consider your budget for your space.

There are two schools of thought on this topic. Some restaurateurs believe you should at least have a preliminary budget on everything before signing a lease because you'll then have a solid plan on every point. Others believe you should find a location first, based on clientele and local appetite, and then adjust expenditures to fit the business model afterward. In actual practice, there is rarely a perfect chronological order to everything. Most loans require documentation of every expense before the money is granted, but it's impossible to know what you can afford until you know what kind of funding you have. It may all seem a circuitous catch-22 of impossibility, but there is one thing you can do to mitigate all of the questions and budgetary concerns: keep researching.

When you search for property, you will likely find listings that include the following:

- Exterior pictures
- Interior pictures
- Address

- Unit number and floor, if applicable
- Square footage
- Existing fixtures (such as kitchen, storage, natural light, street walk-up, restrooms)
- Price per square foot, per year
- Operating expenses

Because commercial spaces are often reconfigured and remodeled, the price is calculated as price per square foot, per year. If a space is advertised as 6000 square feet, and the owner is asking $10 per square foot, per year, the annual rate would be 6000 x 10 = $60,000.

Operating expenses include the costs associated with running a business from that location. Depending on your lease, this may be in addition to rent, or part of the rental price. Unfortunately, operating expenses can become very complicated and involve things outside of your control, such as building occupancy, reconciliation billing, and unexpected jumps when business in the building waxes and wanes. Always inspect the terms and conditions of the operating expenses and ask questions about how it is calculated when looking at a property and discussing with the property owner.

Another consideration that impacts both your budget and the space you choose is profit. This may not seem like an obvious conclusion but consider the entire sales process. Let's look at a coffee kiosk, to start Drive through only. One by one, cars place their order at the speaker and receive their delicious coffee and snacks at the window. The process is efficient, and depending on staffing and machinery, you can serve X number of people per hour. Then let's consider a coffee shop where patrons are encouraged to come in and stick around. They'll need places to sit, as well as a designated place to queue. The space behind the counter has to allow for an efficient flow of business. You'll need plenty of room for baristas to correctly prepare orders as quickly as possible to prevent the flow of customers from creating a traffic jam inside the shop, in the doorway, or in the parking lot. Efficiency and profit go hand-in-hand, and the space you choose must be able to handle the flow of business.

Asking All the Right Questions

Once you've settled all of the location and financial aspects, you'll have your lists narrowed down to some possibilities that make sense on all ends. Now is the time to start following up on those leads! For each one, reach out to the listing agent or party arranging the lease or sale. Be forthright and honest and explain your purpose. They may know of reasons the property might not work well for your coffee shop and will disclose those before you get too invested in the process. They may also know of properties you might not have considered or even be aware of yet, which could equally suit your needs.

Schedule a time to meet with the listing agent or property owner. Come prepared with a list of questions, including the following (some of which may depend on whether you intend to rent or purchase):

1. How long is the standard lease? What is the exact move-in day and exact final date of the lease (unless extended)? If the space is currently occupied, what happens if they aren't out by the exact move-in day?
2. How much is rent or selling price, and what is included? Real estate taxes, operational costs, building maintenance, insurance?
3. When does rent increase, and by how much? While the property owner might not have a set schedule, they should have historical information that demonstrates rent changes in the past.
4. As discussed earlier, what kind of "escape clause" is available, in case something unforeseen should cause you to close the doors? Is subleasing an option?
5. What are the renewal procedures?

6. Can the landlord sell the property during your lease, and if so, what happens to you?
7. What are the insurance requirements for the property?
8. What are the zoning restrictions or provisions for the property?
9. Who are the neighbors? While the location may be prime, it's best to not have a direct competitor right next door. Similarly, you want to be surrounded by businesses that complement or add business to yours, and vice-versa.
10. What about CAM? CAM stands for "common area maintenance" and includes the areas you might share with other businesses, like parking lots, sidewalks, and more.

These are, of course, just a few questions to get you started. You may have additional questions once you get involved in conversation with the agent or landlord, and it's always important to ask questions as they come to mind. Asking now will prevent an ill-fated discovery down the road.

Making "Cents" of Your Space

The next step is viewing the property. If you've done your homework, you've already seen the outside and evaluated the positive and negative aspects of the storefront, parking lot, and overall visibility and access from the road. Now is the time to see what's inside.

Walk through the space at least three times. First, walk through with no expectations—just notice all of the details. What's the natural light like? Where are the vents, speakers, electric sockets? What is the feel of the interior? Are there any fixtures already in place? Where are the restrooms? Is there plumbing and gas jets in place for adding kitchen fixtures?

Next, experience the space in terms of how you want to set it up. Where is the most logical place to put the cash register? The service counter? The espresso machines? Where will the kitchen go? What lighting would be needed to improve visibility? How many tables and chairs can you fit in the space? Is there room for some of the optional features you may have considered, like a bookcase, or a performance area? Take your time with this step. Take measurements, because you'll want to block off space later when creating the final floor plan. It's absolutely critical that the space fits the business, so really consider how things will fit without creating a fire hazard or causing a traffic jam during peak business hours.

Once you've got an idea of where you want to put all of the fixtures, walk through again as if you are a customer. When you walk through the door, what will the customer see? Where does the natural traffic flow direct them? Will they become confused when looking for the restroom? Will there be enough room to wait comfortably for a drink to be prepared? Where do you naturally look to see a menu? Can a menu be placed in that location? Do you have to wander through the restaurant and seating area to form a queue? You may have to revisit these two steps a few times. While you don't want to jeopardize the time of the agent or property owner allowing you this time in their space, take notes, measurements, and pictures so you can reference this location later, if it looks promising.

Once you take this information home, you'll have the ability to create floor plans. This will be the true test to determine if this space will really work. What size and shape will the countertops be? Is there plenty of room for workers behind the counter? Are there any awkward spaces? What can you do to reduce empty space?

You may wish to pull out the graph paper and a pencil, or for a more modern take on designing a floor plan, consider one of the many apps or software options available. These programs allow you to input the dimensions of everything you may need to get a floor plan started. Even better, they often have both mobile and laptop compatibility, meaning you can access your plans anywhere. Consider what fixtures are there, if any. If you are building your own coffee shop from the ground, this obviously won't be applicable, but for those who are purchasing or leasing an existing spot, think about these things:

- What kind of counter space exists?
- What kind of storage exists?
- Are there appliances, or outlets/areas for appliances?
- Are there closets?
- Where are the doors, and do they open inward or outward?
- What about plumbing or sinks? Are they installed, or is there a designated space where these things can be added?

Regardless of whether you are leasing or purchasing a space, you may encounter a fully empty space or the remains of a previous business. If you are leasing, check what kind of allowances and restrictions they allow for adding your own fixtures. What materials can you use? What building permits will you need? Are there any limits or requirements for contractors? These are factors that will impact your budgeting, so this is a very important time to consider what additions or remodeling will be needed.

Looking Out

While the interior is the most important feature of your coffee shop, the exterior is also a significant part of the package. Will you have room for outdoor seating? What does the landscaping look like? If you're leasing, will you have any responsibilities for the landscaping?

What about signage? Much of the size and type of sign you hang to advertise your business depends on local restrictions and regulations; however, take a look at where the sign is in relation to the road. For example, think of many fast-food restaurants, which have large, glowing signs that hover above the roadways, often with marquees that display current specials. If you're looking at a property in a shopping plaza-type setting, is there a directory sign at the entrance, as well as personalized signage near the shop door? Some property owners have requirements on fonts, sizes, and colors involved in signage, so double-check this now to avoid spending money on signs you won't be able to hang.

Depending on the area, you may also want to consider security and privacy gates to protect your glass, your belongings, and your overall business when you're closed. Does the building include—or even permit—these items?

Make Sure It's on the Up-And-Up

As this process develops, you will become intimately familiar with all the legal requirements of zoning, the ADA, the health code, fire code, and all the local requirements and permits that allow you to open your coffee shop. There will be many inspections, and many codes to follow. How will this space stack up to all of these regulations? The property owner or agent may have some details, especially if the space has been used for a similar business in the past, but doing your research is essential to make sure you don't miss out on any important restrictions that might put a damper on your plans. These requirements vary from location to location, so while we can't provide every requirement, we have posted several good resources in the index.

Now that we're diving deeper into all the things to keep in mind when choosing a space, you're probably starting to remove some of the possible locations from your lists, or shuffling them around a bit. When we said earlier that each option is a learning experience, this is exactly what we meant. A space that initially looked promising may end up being cost-prohibitive due to the operational costs, or have a lease that just doesn't make sense for your business. Financial considerations are often the number one deal breaker when it comes to choosing the right spot for your coffee shop, once all of the location needs have been met. Fear not—the right space will appear! You may have to widen your gaze, wait for exactly the right moment to pounce on the perfect property or reconsider your business plan, but this is a land of opportunity!

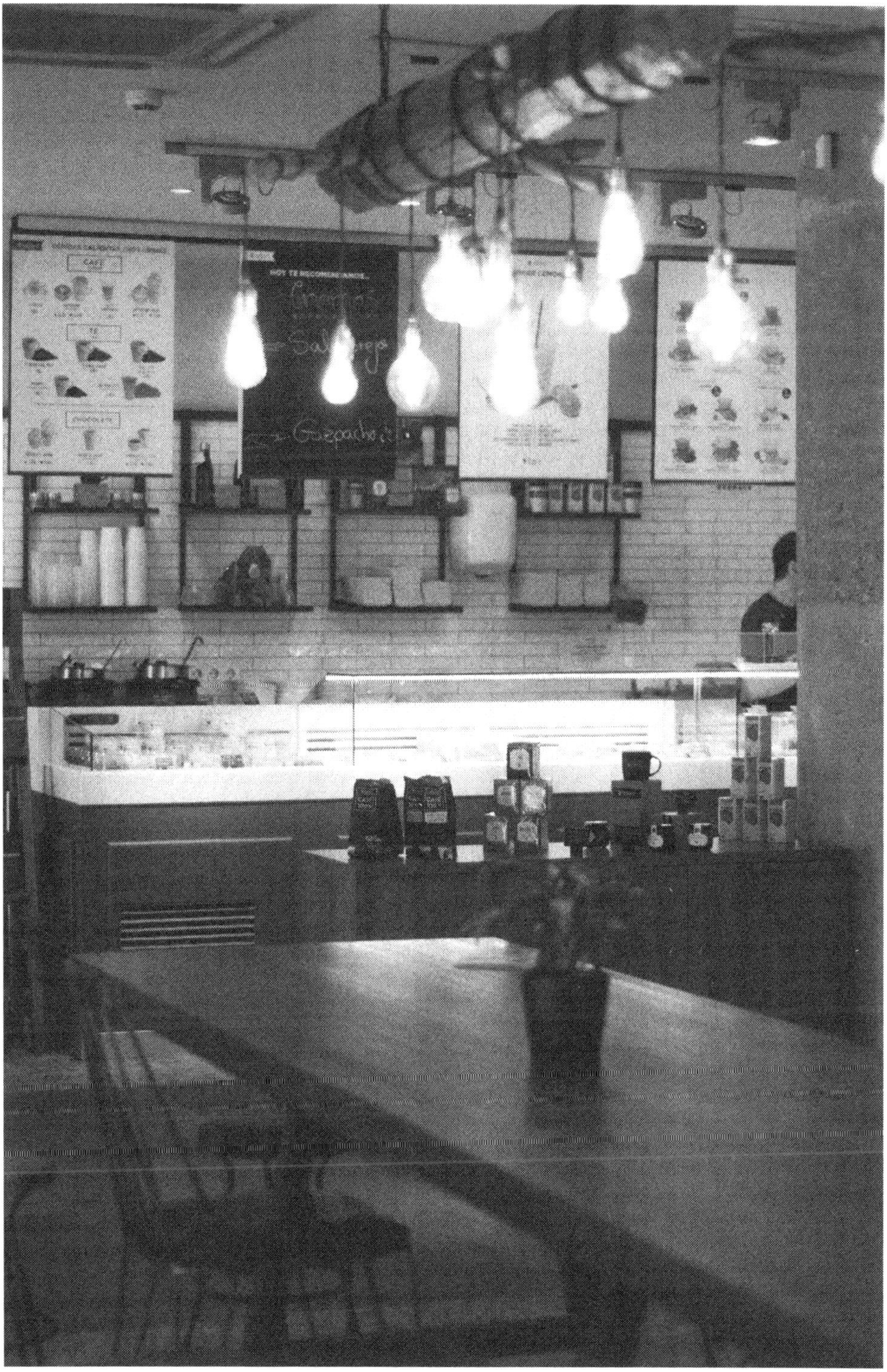

Step 4: Time to Go Shopping

Once you've found the ultimate space for your new coffee shop, it is appropriate to begin the process of filling it. You may have had your eye on a few things here and there while dreaming and doing research, and there's never an inappropriate time to look at your options. It's best to wait to do the actual shopping part once you've established a budget and found a solid location. Often times, it's much easier to purchase something than it is to return it, so waiting until you have firm plans in place is generally going to save you time, and potentially money.

Construction First

As mentioned earlier, you may need to do some remodeling to make the space perfect for your business. The first consideration is how you're going to accomplish that. With your floor plan in hand, determine the actual scope of your project. Are you looking at putting up a couple of shelves, or are you starting from scratch, building all of the countertops, adding electrical outlets, installing flooring, and more?

If you or someone you know well are handy, you might be tempted to take on the construction project yourself. But remember—this is a public business, subject to all sorts of codes and regulations. You'll likely need a permit for your work and have to build to the specifications of all of these regulations. The actual physical construction might be much easier than keeping up with all of the legal requirements! It may be an all-around better idea to hire a contractor for your project.

There are some advantages to hiring an independent contractor to handle your remodeling, as well as some considerations that you'll need to keep in mind. Make a list of the benefits and concerns you might encounter when going with a contractor.

PROS	CONS
Will know the legal requirements	Will be expensive
Could include remodel and design	Might have to adjust timeline
Quality is what you pay for	What if they disappear?
Will bring experience	Less hands-on
Access to larger range of resources	Might have to compromise vision

Your list of pros and cons to hiring a contractor to help you with the construction and remodeling needs in your coffee shop might look different, but these are some general considerations when thinking through the process.

Once you decide to hire a contractor, you'll need to begin the hunt to find one. First, you'll need to thoroughly research highly reputable contractors in your area. Ask family, friends, your landlord, and any trusted party for recommendations and words of caution. Read any local review sites and create a shortlist of preferred contractors. Remember—even though you may have found the perfect contractor, they may not be able to work within your timetable. Having several reliable options will help you find the perfect fit.

You'll also want to have a thorough interview with each contractor. They'll walk through estimates for the project with you, discussing the full scope of what needs to be done. Some contractors work with designers who can help you with the furniture and fixtures, in addition to construction work. This will inevitably be more expensive, but might save you a ton of stress in sourcing these items yourself. As you speak with contractors, it's important to stay true to your vision, but also to admit when you might be out of your depth when it comes to finishing and furnishing your coffee shop space.

Eventually, you will be armed with a handful of estimates and proposals. Do not immediately head for the lowest cost. Make sure the proposals include everything necessary for your project in order to avoid hidden costs. Remember, it is very rare for the estimate to be identical to the final costs of a project, so choosing the most thorough proposal may be the safest route.

As you work with your contractor, remember to be patient, and that good communication is the key to success in any project. Be honest with your self and your contractor when you have concerns, and adhere to your budget at all times. The results will build the threshold to your very own custom coffee shop!

Go with the Flow

Once the stage is set, the next step is to add the furnishings and fixtures that will give it its full appeal. If you've done extensive construction work, you might have a lot of the fixtures already installed at this point. For those who are starting with a space that required little to no remodeling, you'll likely need to purchase everything that goes into your space, so it's time to do some shopping. Actually, it's going to be a LOT of shopping.

The shopping process begins with measurements. Lots and lots and lots of measurements. It's time to bring out the floor plan again, and you may find you need still more measurements. Consider what the interior of your coffee shop will be like when everything is in motion. The floor plan you created is the bigger picture, but now is the time to think about the smaller picture and figure out what you need to keep in mind when putting all of the moving pieces together.

Let's take your refrigerator as an example. Let's say your floor plan works best if you have three smaller refrigerators: one under the counter by the espresso machines, one next to the ice machine, and one in the back. You may be tempted to buy three identical small refrigerators, but they may not all work in their designated spaces. If the refrigerator door is too wide or opens too far, it might bang into another shelving area, or render another piece of equipment unusable, or hold up workers walking by. If the nearest electrical outlet is three feet away, a refrigerator that has a two-foot cord will not work. Taking these seemingly insignificant details into consideration now will save you from a lot of heartache and scrambling for a solution at the last minute.

Much like the staff you eventually hire, all the pieces inside your coffee shop have to work together in harmony. Putting a sofa by the door won't work if the door will constantly slam into the legs of someone sitting there. These are the types of measurements you need to consider when planning your shopping list.

Define Your Style

When you're making your shopping list, it might be easy to write "a sofa" on your list. After the last step, hopefully, that line item has been updated to "a sofa, maximum 6-feet long." In this step, you'll refer back to the business plan to define that even further.

If you are opening a coffee shop in which you expect guests to come in and spend some time, the style of your shop should be cohesive and consistent. It should be inviting, and make people feel comfortable. Customers should want to spend time there.

Your style is your own. Perhaps you want a bohemian feel. Maybe streamlined and stainless steel is your preference. You might be going for that leather-and-mahogany library feel. Whatever your style is, here are some things to keep in mind when adding furniture to your shopping list:

- Customers expect clean furniture. A white velvet sofa may be beautiful, but it will be stained almost instantly. Make sure surfaces can be easily cleaned, stain treated, and meet fire code.

- Customers don't want wobbly furniture. You might find some discount cafe tables online, but make sure they assemble perfectly and provide a level, solid surface.
- Customers will spill. Customers will neglect to use coasters. When considering surfaces on tables, chairs, and the floor, think of what that surface can tolerate. If you put rugs on the floor, how will they get cleaned when a large decaf gets dumped on them? If you purchase wooden tables, are they treated to tolerate moisture, heat, and cold?
- If you have free-standing lamps, how heavy are they? Can they be knocked over easily? Would they cause a serious injury if they fell on a foot, or worse—a child?
- Speaking of children, if you plan to make your establishment child-friendly, can the furniture handle a full load of toys, crayons, markers, and more? If your tables are ruined by a single permanent marker accident, they may not be the best investment for a coffee shop that encourages children to visit.

These are just some things to keep in mind first and foremost. As you build your shopping list for the interior of your coffee shop, you may want to make a line item list that takes all of these pieces into consideration. Be as specific as you need to be!

For example, your shopping list may look like this:

ITEM (QTY)	SIZE	COLOR	NOTES
Sofa/loveseat (2)	6-8 feet long	Maroon, dark brown	Leather sofa, modern style
Coffee Table (2)	4-5 feet long	Dark woodgrain, black	To match sofa, modern style
Cafe Tables (8)	3-foot diameter	Dark woodgrain, black	No more than 36" high, room to seat two guests, round only.
Cafe Seats (16)	Standard, lightweight	Silver/metal	Slatted back, modern look
Bookcase (2)	8 feet tall, 4 feet wide, no deeper than 16 inches	Dark woodgrain, black	Modern look, adjustable shelves, not top heavy—must be solid or wall anchor

In essence, you want your shopping list to include every term you would consider entering in an online search for that object. Add every item that will help your vision come to life, as well as any considerations for ensuring that the item is safe and enjoyable for your environment.

The Big Supplies

Shopping for your new coffee shop extends beyond furniture and appliances, of course. You won't be able to serve customers if you don't have all the supplies you need. This includes everything from cups, lids, and stir sticks, to toilet paper, soap, and floor mats.

You'll need to think through the entire process each time you intend to buy. Not only will you need napkins, you'll need dispensers to hold them. If you're serving food in-house, you'll need not just dishes, but bins to collect dirty dishes, chemicals to wash the dishes, a place to wash dishes, a place to store the dishes, and so on. You may wish to use exclusively disposable service products, including plastic utensils and paper plates, but bear in mind, it will become expensive very quickly. It's also not environmentally friendly, which may alienate some of your customer base.

The kitchen is a very important location for supplies. You'll need chemicals to disinfect all the surfaces, sanitize the dishes, and wash the floors, for example. You'll need handwashing stations, and possibly plastic gloves for food handling. You'll need health department signage hung conspicuously for staff, which is regulated by the state health department. You'll need bar towels to clean up messes, which will also need laundering.

Depending on your location, there may be services that can deliver these items to you on a regular basis. While you may feel confident you can run to the store any time you need more bathroom supplies or napkins, be realistic about your schedule. If you spend all day at the coffee shop, when are you going to feel like getting supplies? When are the stores in your area open? Buying in bulk is always more cost-efficient, so do you have a bulk shop close to you? What membership requirements do they have? Sure, you could probably request a delivery from Amazon or InstaCart in a pinch, but the delivery and service fees aren't necessarily dollars you'll be able to spend at first.

Check the internet for some of the popular companies that provide service in your area, and really take a look at the scope of their services. Some can help with creating logo napkins and to-go cups. Some can wash and replace linens, uniforms, doormats, and stock the bathroom all in one visit. While there will, of course, be fees associated with these services, it's a great idea to do the research and price out what that would cost versus trying to do it all on your own. Sure, you can run to Costco three times a week now, but what happens when you run out of medium cups during a holiday season rush? Peace of mind is difficult to price, so be conscious of your budget and adjust accordingly.

Appliances Big and Small

When considering appliances, there are loads of little details that you may not have considered yet. Sure, you've got a list of what you need, what size, and details like color and plug length, but lots of appliances work a lot of different ways, and all of those functions impact price.

Do you know how much a cafe-style espresso machine costs? The answer is that it can vary, greatly. Depending on how many shots you want to be able to pour at once, you could be looking at hundreds or thousands of dollars. That can mean only one thing—back to the internet for research!

You'll find there are loads of suppliers out there. In fact, many food services offer equipment for sale as well. You can find used equipment, equipment to rent, or choose brand new equipment. Many experienced restaurant owners will caution against used equipment, as it is hard to judge exactly how reliable a used coffee maker may be, for example. It is possible to find great deals, though, so researching these options isn't out of the question. Just be sure to be extra cautious when reviewing any type of appliance. The best value will be a mix of reliability, functionality, safety, and price.

As you shop, also keep in mind that you will need to keep continuous maintenance on every appliance you purchase. Not only does the appliance's dependability rely on it, but health codes may require regular maintenance. Commercial-style refrigerators, for example, can require full cleaning and maintenance that can be very expensive. Before you go all-out on a variety of appliances, consider what you truly need for your first year of business and go from there. Your budget—and your stress level—will thank you.

An Important Reminder and a Second Pep Talk:

Preparing for the opening of your very own coffee shop probably hasn't been a walk in the park so far. You've had to come up with a business plan. You've gone through the rigorous process of financing your operation. It's likely taken you much longer than you anticipated to find just the right location, and you've poured lots of time and money into purchasing all of the right furniture and fixtures for your coffee shop. You may feel a little overwhelmed or discouraged many times throughout the process, but that is entirely normal. There will be good days amongst the bad, and your dreams will eventually come true. One of the wisest statements shared amongst business owners is that, as long as you do something to make progress every single day, even if it doesn't get the results you anticipated, you're still headed in the right direction. Something that may seem small, like hanging a picture on the walls or deciding what you want the countertops to look like, may feel insignificant, but they are still steps toward your Grand Opening.

Step 5: Bringing in the Product

At this point, you've got your location, you've got your seating and appliances, and it's time to make the really, really big decision: What do you serve?

Who You Serve Is What You Serve

One very important rule of thumb in the restaurant business is that what you serve has to match the people who buy it. It's time to revisit the business plan in earnest, especially the section about "Who Is Your Clientele?" Let's walk through a few examples of how who you serve impacts what you serve.

Example A: Your city has a Coffee Festival. You want to be included in this festival. As a result, you'll need to serve the most unique, delicious coffee in the area to gain recognition. You'll want to look at exotic coffees, or perhaps roast your own beans in-house (which means additional equipment, of course!). You're not going to settle for "just whatever;" instead, you're going to search the ends of the Earth to source the most unique coffee. As a result, you'll have a higher price tag than any old neighborhood coffee shop, but you'll have a clientele that is willing to pay for a coffee experience, rather than just a caffeinated drink.

Example B: As a coffee shop that caters to the community, you've decided that you really want to be eco-friendly, which has gained the attention of certain groups in the community. They want to use your coffee shop as a meeting spot, and after spending time with them, you have learned that they appreciate organic and vegan products. In this case, you're going to need to serve plenty of organic coffee options. While you may not serve strictly organic beverages and food, you will want to make sure that you have many choices for these customers.

Example C: You want to build a family-friendly coffee shop, where moms and dads can meet up, and children can interact and have fun. In this case, having exclusive coffee beans isn't nearly as important as having drinks that can be made quickly, thoroughly customized, and are generally inexpensive to create. You'll want a menu that's chock-full of fun drinks for kids, too, perhaps without the espresso. You may look at having more blended drinks, which means an ice maker and lots of milk and not-so-exotic syrups and flavors.

As you can see, the quality and quantity of coffee you purchase depends heavily on who will be doing the drinking. In Example A, you may have smaller quantities of very high-quality coffee. In Example B, you will likely have a substantial amount of tasty organic coffee, but the quality is not nearly as significant as the fact that it is organic. In Example C, the quality of the coffee doesn't matter nearly as much as having plenty of it, backing the sweet zip of caffeine with drink recipes that are imaginative and cater to a wide audience.

A Snack to Suit the Crowd

Any food you may choose to serve will then have to match the coffee. If you're pursuing a gourmet experience, such as in Example A, it would not make sense to have super-basic food. Your customers are going to want a full gourmet experience, so consider pairing this type of coffee with treats that also have that gourmet flair. You may wish to include charcuterie or cheese plates, which can be tasty treat any time of day and coordinated for any meal. You may wish to serve pastries that have a bit of an international flair. Macarons, for example, are a French delight that can be flavored with very high-class ingredients. For those who have an organic-centric menu, such as in Example B, you'll want to continue this commitment and include food options that are organic and vegan. You're going to need organic milk and non-dairy milk options, too. If the patrons of your coffee shop are going to include children, like Example C, you'll want snacks that are easy to hold and easy to clean up. Favorites include cookies, fruit and veggies, or simple sandwiches.

The important thing to remember when creating your menu is that you cannot possibly have everything that every customer wants. Repeat this to yourself many, many times:

> *I cannot run a business that provides everything everyone wants every time.*

It's strictly impossible. Sure, it's great to offer gluten-free, dairy-free, nut-free, and vegan options. But your budget will suffer if you try to make sure you have every version of every dish. If you have carrot, blueberry, and oat muffins, you may wish to carry blueberry muffins in a gluten-free option as well. At some point, someone will be disappointed that you do not have a gluten-free carrot muffin. While the customer's frustration is understandable, you simply cannot carry absolutely everything all at once. You can't store it. You can't order it week after week in hopes that someone will want it. Above all, you can't afford to waste it.

When you're brainstorming recipes, try to use ingredients several times. For example, if you plan on offering a cafe mocha, you'll need chocolate syrup. That same chocolate syrup can be used in countless signature drinks, as topping on blended or iced drinks, as an ingredient in chocolate milk or hot cocoa, and so on. Always use your imagination when coming up with your menu, but try to work with as few unique ingredients as possible. This will save you in many ways: you won't have to store as many products. You won't have to buy as many products. And most of all, you won't have to waste as many products.

So, let's say you really want to create a frozen chocolate and banana drink. Whether you use real bananas or banana-flavored syrup, you'll have to buy that in addition to the chocolate, coffee, and milk. Now let's say you sell one of those drinks each day. Now check the expiration date on the syrup, or glumly watch the bananas languish and turn brown. If you incorporate that banana taste in several other drinks, it won't be wasted, and the cost will make sense for your business model!

Considering the Overall Menu

When first starting your coffee shop, it's really best to keep it simple. Doing a few things very well is going to attract far more customers than doing a lot of things frantically. Every recipe you concoct is going to require not only ingredients, but also time to make it, time to serve it, and time to train staff how to make it. And remember this very important idea: You can ALWAYS add more. As time goes by and your business flourishes, you'll get an even better idea for what customers love. Maybe some interesting frequent drink orders will make it onto the menu as regular offerings. Don't exhaust your creativity before you even open your doors. Start simple with some guaranteed crowd pleasers, and perhaps a handful of signature drinks. That creativity will be your ultimate tool in helping business continue to flourish as the customer base grows!

Make your menu flexible, as well. Each customer is going to have different tastes, dietary requirements, and possible allergies. Consider possible add-ons, like an extra flavor shot, specialty milk, adding cheese to a sandwich, and more. What options and upgrades will you provide? What will you charge for these upgrades? Don't go overboard with the options, but make it flexible, so that the customer who can't have dairy can order almond milk, or so the customer who doesn't like banana but loves caramel can have that instead. This is not in contradiction to the earlier advice regarding having too many options, but adjacent to it. You are not adding options to your menu, you are simply replacing one thing with another thing you have in stock already.

Sourcing Coffee

Where will you find your coffee? It may seem that the options are endless. A Google search will lead you down a rabbit hole of options, but it is a very good way to get a feel of some of the available choices. At the same time, you may have a few good resources closer to your coffee shop.

Some coffee shops roast their own beans. This means you'll have to find a source of raw coffee beans and the equipment for roasting, as well as the knowledge and expertise in the roasting process, which is a little more in-depth than watching a YouTube video a few times. Unless you already have this experience, you may want to work your business up to this process.

Perhaps you have a local coffee roaster in your city or state. If you enjoy their product and it fits with your business model, you may wish to reach out to them regarding their wholesale capabilities. Please note that while many roasters will be thrilled by the opportunity, some smaller businesses may simply lack the capacity to produce regular large orders. As you work with this roaster, you'll agree upon a price, transport of the beans from their business to yours, and any cross-promotion or marketing you'll do for each other. You've likely seen signs that state "Proudly Serving (Brand)" at various coffee shops, which is an indication that the proprietor is doing the exact same thing.

Lastly, there are wholesale opportunities, even for gourmet coffee! Many food services offer upscale coffee, but there are several companies dedicated specifically to supplying coffee shops and venues that specialize in coffee. Take a look at some of these options when making your sourcing decisions, because you will likely find a few tasty beans which you might not have even thought about! Additionally, these services have serious expertise, and while you'll be paying a higher amount to have their roasted beans delivered to you, this can be extremely cost-effective in the long run, especially when first starting out.

Creating Vs. Assembling Vs. Purchasing

Once you've finalized the menu, it's time to figure out how the treats you've decided upon are going to make it from your imagination to the customer's hands. The three most popular models for adding food to your menu are Creating, Assembling, and Purchasing. Some coffee shops use one model exclusively, while others use a little bit of each method. Here are a few of the things to consider about each option:

- Creating means baking from scratch. If you choose this method, you'll need:
- Recipes
- All of the ingredients
- Storage for the ingredients
- Equipment for stirring, mixing, baking, etc.
- Room for laying out ingredients, mixing, and putting together baking sheets
- A staff member to have baking completed by opening. Typically, a baker will work overnight to ensure the products are as fresh as possible by the time your doors open for the day.

Naturally, all of these elements have practical and financial considerations. Buying and storing ingredients such as flour, sugar, and butter, is very inexpensive and simple, and these individual ingredients typically have a long shelf life. This translates into less waste. At the same time, you'll have to pay a staff member to come in for a few hours every night to make the goodies. You'll have to make sure they're trained and properly equipped.

Assembling means you'll have pieces and parts of your menu items on hand, which can be put together or heated upon request. You'll need:

- Each piece of the item for assembly. For example, if you want to have Danish on the menu, you could purchase frozen pastry shells and filling.
- Room to assemble
- The equipment to combine ingredients or bake, which could include ovens, pans, sandwich presses, or soup urns

These are going to be more expensive and require more slightly more intense storage than dry ingredients, with a shorter shelf life, but you'll have the ability to make each product to order, which will help keep waste down. You'll also be able to quickly train staff to assemble each treat according to your specifications, so there will be no need for an additional staff member.

Lastly, there's always the option to purchase your treats. Some coffee shops prefer working with local bakeries or eateries to bring in their products daily. This could range from having this other business make all of the food for your coffee shop, or perhaps just elements, for example, loaves of bread. Contracting with local companies is a great way to establish yourself in the community. By carrying a brand name that is already known and loved, the customers of that brand will be intrigued by your new enterprise. You and the other business owner can cross-promote and host events together, which will be a very fun and simple way to gain business in your community.

Another option for purchasing treats is to check out the offerings of wholesale food retailers. Perhaps your supply service also offers gourmet treats, which can be stored, refrigerated or frozen (depending on type and ingredients), and served with little to no preparation. This is going to be the most expensive option at the outset because you're purchasing a fully prepared product. These items will likely have a very short shelf life since they're ready to eat, but you most likely won't need any supplies other than perhaps a microwave oven to briefly thaw or reheat the item.

When purchasing your food, you'll either sell out very quickly, or experience a significant amount of waste. You'll also need more space for refrigeration, which as you may recall from the earlier section, requires a great deal of maintenance and attention to keep it up to health code. Some restaurant owners report that keeping a walk-in cooler fully compliant can cost several thousand dollars each inspection period. When factoring in the high cost of ready to eat food, plus the cost of adequate refrigeration, you'll likely have very little room for profit, or be forced to charge a significant amount more than customers are willing to spend.

Regardless of which option you choose, you will need to find a supplier for your food or ingredients. Some areas are lucky enough to have a local restaurant wholesaler, which will allow you to peruse the stock and get a feel for the taste and quality of their products before committing to a regular order. If not, have no fear—there are a variety of national companies that supply restaurants nearly everywhere.

As with every other purchase you've made, you'll need to do a lot of research and a little shopping around for the best options and deals. Value is, again, not just choosing the least expensive option. The best option may not be the most expensive. Evaluate everything not only by price, but by how easy or difficult it is to store it, how labor intensive it is to produce it, and of course, how good it tastes.

One very important hint that chefs around the world swear by is to Taste Everything. Don't sell
something unless you can personally vouch for its taste and quality. Furthermore, don't just taste it yourself. Taste is hugely subjective, so invite friends and family to help you with taste tests. You may repeat these tests more than once, so gather a group of people with very different taste buds and preferences!

Tasting things helps you decide exactly how to make them in a manner that most customers will enjoy. You will need to refine your recipes down to the quantity of each ingredient for each item made, so make sure that you have the perfect amount of flavor syrup, the perfect water-to-bean ratio, the right fineness when grinding beans, the most delicious filtered water, and the right number of blueberries in your scones. Quantity translates into inventory, so consider the cost of each ingredient when adding it to your recipes.

You may be very tempted to choose the cheapest option on the market, and sometimes, that might be perfectly fine. Often, things like sugar packets or non-dairy creamer are roughly the same no matter which brand or supplier you choose.

There are many instances, however, in which quality is required. If your baked goods taste dry because you bought them on the "day old" rack, no one will buy them, and your reputation will suffer. If your coffee tastes burnt, you'll sell less of it. If your blended drinks aren't sweet enough, or no one can actually taste the banana in your chocolate-banana drink, it's not good enough to sell. Don't cut corners—create a menu that is lively, and that offers quality that matches both the experience and the price. This is yet another way you can avoid waste.

On the Topic of Waste

Waste is a very common and unavoidable topic when serving food or beverages of any kind. There are many ways in which waste can occur, and it may not be something you can prevent. Here are some of the most common forms of waste:

Preventable waste:
- Serving the customer the wrong product
- Having more inventory than you can sell
- Improper storage
- Improper handling

Unpreventable waste:
- Customer tries the product but doesn't like it
- Power outage
- Accidentally spilling, dropping, overheating, or otherwise making the product unsaleable
- Spoiling too soon or arriving damaged

As you can see, waste can happen even under the best intentions. If you are familiar with any type of produce, you'll know that there is always the chance that the apples or grapes will go bad long before you expect them to. Food simply isn't designed to be limitless, so you will find yourself throwing out food despite storing and handling everything properly.

At the same time, there are some very definite steps you can take to ensure you aren't swimming in waste. Try to be scrupulous when ordering inventory, for example. The general rule about inventory is that you won't have it perfected until your third year of business. When starting out, you are literally going to be guessing about quantities and amounts of everything. You'll learn a little more each month, and certain patterns will slowly start to reveal themselves. In the food industry, almost every single business owner will confess that they've had to run to the local grocery store at some time in their career due to running out of an essential item.

Remember, it is far more cost effective to run out of a product, apologize, and offer the customer a similar item, than it is to throw away large quantities of stock because it didn't sell.

When creating your recipes, be specific about amounts, and make sure you have the equipment to help your future staff measure correctly. If your recipe says "6 ounces of milk," make sure they know how much 6 ounces really is, either with measuring cups, or marked cups used specifically for measuring. Don't switch it up, either: if your recipe calls for 2 ounces of syrup, don't tell workers, "that's, like, two or three pumps." Consistency reduces waste. If every drink and food item is made the exact same way every single time, barring accidents, the customer will receive identical product every single time, and you'll be able to accurately measure how much of each product you're using daily.

Additionally, it's important to pay attention to the rules you'll learn when earning your ServSafe certification. This required certification for those serving and handling food items will help you gauge the best ways to store, assemble, create, and serve any food and beverage your coffee shop sells. Health code adherence will also teach you some important things, such as how quickly the steamed milk should be cooled, which products can be left out of the refrigerator for how long, and which products have the potential to make many people very sick.

At this point, you'll have your stack of drink and food recipes in one hand, and your budget in the other. While we have provided some handy references in the index, this list is not exhaustive. Depending on your location and network, you may have many more resources available to you. Creativity is a necessity when it comes to owning a business, as you have likely learned by now. Find multiple solutions for each supply requirement, and soon you'll have put together all of the pieces that make up your supply chain.

Step 6: The Wild World of Marketing

Sure, there are marketing geniuses out there, but many smaller businesses, especially those who cater to a smaller community rather than the whole wide world, are perfectly capable of handling marketing in-house. Marketing has a reputation for being a bit of a wild world, perhaps due to the ever-changing landscape of what's in, what's out, what's trending, what's now considered passe, etc. Do not allow yourself to become paralyzed by fear at the word "marketing."

If you have already started spreading the word in the community, you've already started marketing. If you have a sign outside your location that says "Coming soon..." you've already started marketing. See? That wasn't so hard! The next few steps will take a little strategy and attention, but don't worry—the internet is absolutely flooded with helpful guides to marketing. Here are our very simple rules for researching marketing on the internet:

- DO: Research one topic at a time.
- DO: Take notes or print off any step-by-step guides.
- DON'T: Go down the rabbit hole. Everything you read will link to twenty other topics. Stay on task.
- DON'T: Take everything as a law. Red may be THE color for this season, but in two weeks, blue might suddenly be the attention color. These are not rules, they are suggestions.

That being said, here are some helpful hints for various marketing avenues that you may wish to pursue in order to give your new coffee shop the attention it needs. It is highly recommended that you start the marketing process well before you open your doors. Build excitement and anticipation for your new business!

Sign Here

Signage is very important. It tells people where your shop is located. It sets the very first impression of your shop. Your logo and sign are your very first communication with your future customers, so make it count. Choose fonts and colors that truly represent your coffee shop, and that match your vision and plan. For example, if you're looking to establish a gourmet experience, you won't want signage in Comic Sans. Instead, you'll want images and fonts that convey a truly elegant location.

The size of your signage and logo are also important. Simple names and logos can be printed in a variety of sizes, even quite small. Think of some of the most iconic logos of our time. Even if you were to see the McDonald's Golden Arches printed the size of this text, you would still associate it with the fast-food restaurant. A more complicated logo, however, will lose focus as it becomes smaller, with intricate details getting kicked out as the pixel count decreases. Make sure your sign is readable, and that your logo doesn't turn into a smudge when viewed from afar, or in a smaller format.

You may wish to hire a designer to help you nail down the details of your logo, especially if you're feeling less than artistic. There are also many websites that can help you with this process. Granted, you'll need to tap into the budget once again, but many online logo services are reasonably priced, and will help you build a lasting logo that will help your business become readily recognizable for years to come.

Www. You're Going to Build a Website. Com

In this day and age, creating a website is an inevitable requirement for nearly every business. People will hear your business name, and they'll head to their smartphone to look up important information like hours of operation, days that you're open, and an idea of what you serve. This is reasonable information to request, and it makes sense to give the people what they need. After all, you want to give them absolutely every reason to show up for fresh scones at 6 am on Monday morning!

There are tons of ways to create websites, but perhaps one of the most popular and easy-for-nearly-everybody site builders is WordPress. WordPress is inexpensive, it's popular, it includes a lot of freebies to help you get started, and it involves really simple aspects like drag-and-drop images and videos.

Whatever platform you choose for your website, you can decide to be as elaborate as you want; however, there are certain factors which you need to have displayed in a way that customers can very clearly find them, even when they are under-caffeinated and blearily making their way to your parking lot. These include:

- Your logo
- What kind of business you are
- Your address
- Your hours of operation
- A few pictures
- A page which displays a menu
- (example: http://www.riverroadcoffeehouse.com/)

When adding photos and content to your website, there are a few things to keep in mind. First, you want all content to be "evergreen." That means that for the most part, you will rarely have to change this content, if ever. Things like your photo and biography are evergreen. Your address and any Google map link you choose to add to it won't change. When uploading menu information, make sure you include top sellers and products you plan to offer continuously. You are more than welcome to update your website with the "Special of the Week" or the "Pastry of the Day," but remember, that means you will have to update that information every time it changes, or you'll gain a reputation for having an out-of-date website.

Using your own images is always the safest option, and in this day of smartphones with built-in cameras, it is extremely easy. While you may yearn for those beautiful, fine-tuned photos you see on the websites of more established websites, you'll have to make sure you have it in your budget to hire a professional photographer. You may wish to incorporate some images taken by other professionals into your website but beware: most photographers or businesses have copyrighted their photos, which means you absolutely cannot use them to promote your business without permission. Stock photos are an option, and frequently free or very inexpensive. Always give credit where credit is due, so if you incorporate another party's image, make sure you give them photo credit.

Having an out-of-date website can be a problem for a few reasons. First, customers won't like it. They'll completely call you out if the Pastry of the Day has been a pistachio muffin for six months. Secondly, it reflects poorly on you as a business owner. Visitors to your website will wonder what's wrong with business that you don't have time to change a single line of text (which makes it worth mentioning—many sites, including WordPress—can be accessed via your mobile). They may question the reliability of other information on your website, including hours of operation, and decide not to stop by. Lastly, these types of inaccuracies can reflect poorly on your Google ratings. If people go to your website and get incorrect information, they'll stop going to your website. If they stop going to your website, it will become buried under other local options, so when folks in your area search for "coffee shop near me," your shop will not be at the top of the list. You definitely want to be at the top of the list!

"Stellar content!" is one of the most popular marketing battle cries, and for good reason. Your website is absolutely worthless if the content isn't intelligent, entertaining, and full of accurate information. There are several ways you can communicate content to folks through your website, and how deep you want to go depends on your overall goals for your business. Note: You do not have to give these pages the specific names—these are categories, more than titles! Be yourself!

1. An "About" page. For most businesses, having an About page is a great idea. Not only does this allow people to read more and linger on your page, which drives up those Google ratings, but it gives people an idea of who you are, and what your business is about. It humanizes you and personalizes the experience for all your customers. You don't have to go into a great deal—typically, 300-500 words is enough.
2. An "Experience" page. This page will tell the audience what to expect when they walk into your coffee shop. "When you walk into my coffee shop, your senses will be enrobed in the aroma of fresh-brewed coffee from around the world." This is where you can paint a picture of your vision to share with people and draw them in. Make them think they can't possibly pass up on your coffee! Tell them whose beans you sell, or your roasting process. Get them as excited as you are about your coffee shop.
3. An "Events" page. This is only important if you are going to actually host events or happenings at your coffee shop, but it can be useful for attracting attention to anything fun that might draw a larger crowd. If you're having a paint night, for example, let people know. If the local Kiwanis will be there every Thursday night, put it on the calendar. The benefit of this is that people will be able to pick a great time to experience your coffee shop and know when might not be the best time. If the Kiwanis are meeting, a harried mother may not want to drag the entire soccer team to your shop after practice, for example.
4. A Menu. You can either post your menu as an image or link to a PDF folks can download. As mentioned earlier, you might want

to make this relatively non-specific, especially at first, when you're finding what works best for your business. Adding simple things like "House Blend - a delicious 100% Kenyan blend, roasted at nearby place" will suffice, as well as the price per size. If you're not fully sure what specific pastries you'll have on hand, "A rotating selection of fine treats and snacks—ask your barista for more information!" will be perfect. If you don't serve food at all, this is also a great time to mention it, so that someone who has a hankering for a snack doesn't let loose their hanger (that's their anger from hunger) on you!

5. A Blog. Now we're getting into some of the more elaborate functions, but there are a couple of really good reasons you might want to feature a blog on your website, especially before opening.

   a. First, that content will set the scene for prospective customers. Yes, you've painted a pretty picture in the "Experience" page, but the blog is a journey. You can post about how exciting it was, trying to source the perfect beans. You can post pictures of the entire process of setting up the space. You are basically telling the story of your coffee shop here. You are explaining to your audience the who, when, where, what, and how of the entire vision and plan that you started with in the very first step. This draws them in and makes them more emotionally and personally invested in your coffee shop.

   b. Next, a blog improves Google ratings. The more time someone spends on your website, the higher the Google rating!

   c. Having this information made public will also gain attention. As chatter spreads about your upcoming Grand Opening, you might have the media reach out to you, including local websites, newspapers, groups, etc. By having accurate information prominently displayed on your website, you have already taken the first step in revealing yourself to the community, and this information might be featured in any media reports about your location.

d. Social media crossover. We're about to talk more about social media, but one very nice feature of blog posts is that you can link to them from any other social media, so, instead of having to write several different posts each time you update social media, you can simply write, "Check out our latest blog post here!" with a link. Easy as can be!

e. Make sure your social media links are also posted on your website, too. Make it as easy as possible for people to find every shred of information they may wish to discover about your shop!

Follow Us On…

Nearly everyone and their grandmother can be found on some level of social media these days. Facebook, Instagram, and Twitter seem to be the "big three" of this decade, but given the fickle nature of social media, that could change in an instant. For now, let's focus on using social media in a constructive way… though maybe not an "out of the box creative" way.

Let's start with Facebook. Having a business page on Facebook takes a little bit of patience to set up, but once you do, you'll be able to start networking, advertising, and drawing in the community right away! The beauty of Facebook is that you can post all sorts of things to gain the attention of your community—photos, text, videos, events, and more. People can comment and interact with your posts, which will bump them up in the mysterious Facebook algorithm so that more and more people see your posts. People will also be able to share your posts with each other, drawing more and more followers to your page.

To start your brand new Facebook page, visit www.facebook.com/business. From there, you'll be asked all kinds of questions about your business. Answer these questions honestly, as the information you provide will be published in the profile of your page. This is important because people trying to learn more about your business will land there. Make it easy for them!

Next, you'll want to upload some pictures. Your logo makes a great user pic. A picture of your storefront or sign makes an excellent cover photo. Since you're establishing a coffee shop, add a bunch of pictures that are rich in coffee content.

Now what about content? Obviously, you will want to mention as many times as possible when you plan to open. You will want to make it abundantly clear where you are located, and what you serve. Just like the landing page of your website, you don't want people to have to search for clues.

At the same time, you'll want to be engaging. Sticking within the theme and vision of your coffee shop, consider posting memes about coffee, links to news articles about coffee, videos that explain some of the ins and outs of coffee that your regular drinker might not know. Inform. Educate. Entertain. The goal is to have people share your posts with other people, which will gain more exposure for you and your coffee shop!

What about Instagram? Instagram is all about the pictures. Chances are high that you won't update this account as frequently as your Facebook. There is no perfect frequency of updates that will magically create the perfect number of customers. A lot of it depends on your community, your audience, and how you network. However, posting quality content to Instagram is just as important. You don't have to be a professional photographer to get attention on Instagram; besides, the most important part is gathering followers.

Twitter can be harder to master for new initiates. With its shorter word count and compressed messages, as well as a constantly moving tide of trending topics, it's hard to stay on top of what's important on Twitter. Don't despair, though: one easy trick on Twitter is linking the photos you use on Instagram or the posts you make on Facebook to your Twitter account. This will keep your feed constantly refreshed without having to count letters and characters. You can also link to any specials or blog posts that you include on your website.

So how do you get followers? One tried-and-true method is to start with the people you already know. Send requests to all of your friends and family. Even if they don't live in the same community, they can pass on the link to your accounts to their friends and family. This is the very basic formation of a network.

Next, link up with local or community Facebook groups. Does your town have a restaurant owners' group? How about local foodie groups? Any community bulletin board groups? Some neighborhoods have their own Facebook groups, and many would love to hear about a new coffee shop in their area. Linking up with groups will expand your visibility past friends and into the community.

What about Facebook ads? Boosting a post on Facebook is relatively inexpensive, and you have the option of setting demographic specifications when doing so. This is a true case of "you get what you pay for," because Facebook will explain exactly how many days and how many people will be able to see your ad, based on the ad level you purchase. There's no guarantee that all of those people will care, or that any of those people will appear at your coffee shop, looking to try your delicious beverages. It's not a bad idea to boost your posts once in a while, as long as you can afford the audience range you really want. At minimum, Facebook users will see your logo in their feed, which may eventually lead them to check out your shop.

Important Things to Avoid on Social Media

Since so many people are on social media in some capacity, you will likely encounter some troublesome individuals and some uncomfortable situations. As a business owner, it is most beneficial for the overall success of your business that your social media accounts are a neutral place. That means you must present the cleanest, most un-opinionated material possible. That means:

- No politics
- No controversial current events (unless unavoidable—such as a road closure that will impact your business)
- No arguing or engaging with argumentative customers. When people say rude, obnoxious, or obviously inflammatory comments on your page, we strongly recommend taking those conversations out of the public eye. In fact, if you can convince that individual to call you directly, even better. It's important to address their concerns (unless absolutely off-the-wall), but doing so in the public eye, where screenshots can spread like wildfire, is an incredibly bad idea.
- No inappropriate language or images
- No bad-mouthing the competition
- Stay positive at all times

Once you become a community mainstay, you might begin to feel a little too comfortable with your internet family. Avoid doing anything that might be construed as controversial, and you should have no problems navigating a successful social media presence.

The Method of Our Forefathers

One of the most timeless methods of marketing is just getting out there, physically. Having an actual physical presence is more than just putting up a few "Coming Soon" signs or hanging your official store sign. You need to advertise more than out of the corner of someone's eye as they drive by.

Consider printing up flyers with your logo, your address, and Grand Opening information. Depending on your local ordinances, there are many ways you can distribute these amongst your community to let them know that your business is coming soon. Some establishments may allow you to hang small posters announcing your opening. Never assume that businesses will allow your flyers or posters—always ask before hanging.

As we mentioned in the section regarding funding options, getting out into the neighborhood via events and gatherings is a great idea. You also may wish to join the local Chamber of Commerce, or business association, or one of many possible groups in which local business owners network and discuss current events. Becoming acquaintances with other local business owners prior to opening will help you gain a welcome entry into the community, and you may use these connections to your favor in the future.

All the Right Stuff

Then there's the matter of merchandising. Proudly displaying your logo in your community is a great idea, but where's the sweet spot of "stuff"?

When it comes to merchandising, one of the most popular items businesses sell are logo t-shirts. These are pretty simple to acquire, as there are many sites across the internet that will allow you to upload your logo, and for a fee, print your logo on a variety of merchandise. This fee can vary greatly, depending on the type and quantity of merchandise. The rules may be different for different shops. Some base your order on total number of items ordered (say, 14 t-shirts and 14 mugs), while others have bulk pricing per type of item.

At first, you may wish to purchase very little merchandise. While it's a great moneymaker, chances are low that people will buy a t-shirt from an unestablished business. At the same time, if you're purchasing a bunch of logo shirts for your staff, for example, purchasing a few extra will likely bring the price-per-shirt down. The same is true if you're making logo coffee mugs for your shop. Adding a few to the count might offer you a better price on your overall order, which you can recoup by selling them to customers in your shop.

Generally speaking, small items are a safe bet. Things like stickers or decals, even pins or buttons are inexpensive when bought in bulk and can be handed out or sold to customers. These items take up very little room, as well, so you won't sacrifice much storage or display space, either. Make sure that whatever merchandise you invest in can be neatly displayed, can be stored in a clean, safe place, and carries a level of interest to your customers. Sure, it might be fun to have skateboards with your logo printed on them, but do you or your customers actually need a skateboard? (If skating is your theme, then of course, that might be a "yes"!)

The goal of marketing is to get your name into the public, excite and draw in customers, and establish a positive reputation in your community. These suggestions are hardly exhaustive; if anything, they should inspire you to think of other options that will help you connect your community with the business you will soon be opening.

As the years go by, your marketing plan may change and develop. Trends may be very different two years from now, so one important factor in a successful marketing plan is flexibility. At some point, you may wish to consult with a professional, depending on how quickly your business grows. On the other hand, your business might be designed to stay small and local. Every community is different, and there may be some ways to announce your business that are unique to your area. In order to build a brand in your area, you will have to become a part of the neighborhood. A successful marketing program will make your brand, your logo, and your coffee shop familiar to as much of your town or city as possible. As word spreads, the number of customers who visit your shop will increase. They, in turn, will mention the positive experience they have had at your coffee shop with their friends, family, coworkers, and neighbors. Before long, you'll be the talk of town, as everyone stops by to check out the "new kid on the block." These first few months will be intense, and very important for making first impressions amongst your customer base. You will want to put on your best face, so to speak, in every element of your business.

Step 7: The Hiring and Staffing Process

An Important Note about Labor Laws

Before we get started with this chapter, we'd like to mention that there are a lot of legal considerations that go into the staffing process. There are federal employment regulations and state employment regulations. These laws and regulations can cover everything from how often employees must go on break, to how many hours they can work per week. There are things like taxes, workers' compensation, unemployment payments, and who is legally permitted to work for you, all of which must be considered during the hiring process. There will be forms to fill out, all of which bear mysterious, non-specific numeral names, like I9, W2, 1099, and more.

The hiring and staffing process is one in which you can get into a lot of trouble by disobeying the laws. Something as simple as failing to display current labor laws in a prominent area accessed by all staff can earn you serious fines that can jeopardize your coffee shop's ability to stay open. We strongly recommend not taking any chances with fumbling any of these legalities. There are resources that are well-versed in the law, including Human Resources consultants or lawyers, to ensure that any practices you are following throughout this process are 100% legal. At the very minimum, you will need to:

- Obtain an Employee Identification Number (EIN) from the IRS
- Register with your State Department of Labor
- Sign up for Workers' Compensation Insurance
- Set up a payroll system that will withhold taxes
- Make yourself familiar with all the laws that impact your business and your employees, including Title VII of the Civil Rights Act of 1964, The Age Discrimination in Employment Act of 1967, The Americans with Disabilities Act of 1990, and The Family Medical Leave Act of 1993

Knowing the legalities of employment won't make the process any easier, but you will be able to rest, knowing that you are working within the requirements of the law.

When it comes to hiring new personnel, you might feel a bit anxious. The idea of interviewing a stream of strangers, some of whom may be perfectly suited for your coffee shop, and some who may be perfect for a job somewhere else, can be very stressful. You'll have to attract applicants, review resumes, conduct interviews, and train these individuals to run your coffee shop, and after all you've been through getting to this point, you may feel low on energy. That being said, being organized and clear about your vision and plan at this point will serve you just as well as it has in all of the previous steps.

Determine Who Does What … and When

The absolute first step of hiring is figuring out the actual tasks that you need your employees to complete, every single day. Sit down and honestly consider who is going to be doing every single task in your coffee shop. This can include:

- Cleaning machines
- Cleaning the space, including floors, seating areas, restrooms, kitchens
- Collecting trash and taking it to the outdoor receptacle
- Collecting dishes
- Washing dishes
- Restocking supplies
- Taking orders
- Cashing out customers
- Operating age-sensitive machinery, such as slicers and ovens
- Making hot drinks

- Making cold or frozen drinks
- Serving food and beverages
- Baking any food made in-house
- Roasting coffee beans, if done in-house
- Taking inventory
- End of day accounting, including tallying receipts
- Payroll

And possibly much more, depending on the size and scope of your coffee shop. There should never be a moment in which your staff asks you "who is supposed to ____?"

As you get a feel for all of the tasks that have to be completed, both simultaneously and within the course of a business day, you may see that some tasks can be grouped together. For example, the person who is cleaning the dining area could also gather and wash the dishes. The person who is doing end-of-day accounting could also take inventory. This is the process through which you start establishing roles.

In many establishments, many of the roles are interchangeable. For example, many small restaurants and coffee shops have checklists of tasks that need to be accomplished throughout the day, which can be done by any staff member, so long as those tasks are completed in a timely manner. When it comes to emptying trash, any staff member should be able to remove the garbage bag, place it in the collection bin, and replace the trash bag. When it comes to wiping down tables or countertops, most staff members could handle that.

At the same time, there are going to be roles which require more training. The staff members who make drinks are going to need to be trained to memorize all of your various drink recipes. If you are making food from scratch, you'll need a baker who can reliably recreate recipes over and over again. The person who operates the register will have to learn the ins-and-outs of the Point of Sale system. You may wish to have only the most trustworthy employee—perhaps a manager—handle accounting and inventory.

There are, of course, distinct advantages to cross-training absolutely every employee. In smaller establishments, everyone knows how to navigate the cash register and take an order, everyone knows where all the supplies are, and everyone can at least find and follow the drink guide in order to make beverages for guests. Cross-training all of your employees is the best way to ensure you're not left in a lurch when someone is unavailable for a shift.

At the same time, it can be beneficial to create specific roles, specifically in the case of a manager role. Unless you plan to be at your coffee shop every hour of every day, you will need someone to supervise the actions at your shop. You will need a trusted resource that can answer (or find the answer to) any questions, who can confidently reduce conflict, and who can address customer concerns according to company policy on your behalf. A manager can act as your assistant in a variety of ways, which will take some of the burden of daily operations off of you so you can concentrate on keeping your business running smoothly from a budget, marketing, and product perspective.

The number of staff you hire and their roles is entirely up to you and based largely on your coffee shop and your goals, but bear in mind that budget is a part of the equation.

Hire Carefully and Confidently

Once you have established the various roles your employees will have, you'll also have an idea of how many employees you'll need on the floor at any given time. Then consider your operating hours. If your doors are open from 6 am to 9 pm, you'll have to divide up the shifts, as very few people want to work fifteen-hour days. How many shifts will you have, and how many employees per shift? It may not be the same across the board, either. This is something you might not know until you've been in operation for a while. For example, mornings might be an incredible rush, so staffing will need to be at a peak, while evenings are slower and more sedate, requiring fewer staff members. These will be things to keep in mind when planning how many staff members you'll need to hire.

In addition, you'll need to give employees a few days off per week. No one wants to work every day, and in some places, there are laws prohibiting it. So now, you'll want to calculate how many shifts you have, over how many days, and how you'll want to spread employees over those days. Again, there's no right answer, and much of this will depend on employment regulations in your area. You may be required to give employees a break after so many hours on the job, so keep things like this in mind when considering how the schedule will work.

Now you'll have an idea of how many people you need to hire to fill those shifts. One word of the wise when starting out is to hire lean, but not TOO lean. Understaffing means overworking, which leads to employees quitting out of frustration. Set the expectation early in the hiring process that you are a brand new business, and that more employees will be hired as required, but don't dangle that particular carrot in front of your staff for too long. Many people will be understanding, and as long as they are treated well and compensated for their efforts, will help put in the hard work that gets a new business up and running. At the same time, everyone has a breaking point, and "helping out" doesn't mean "running ragged."

What about salaries? Granted, this depends a great deal on the cost of living in your area. You will need to research the wage structure of nearby coffee shops in order to be competitive. You will also need to balance what you can afford to pay staff with your overall budget and monthly expenses. How about tips? Will you have a tip jar available, and if so, how will staff members split tips? You want a system that treats all workers fairly, so be careful. Lastly, what about raises and incentives? Perhaps you offer a holiday bonus for working during what are surely hectic times. You may choose to have incentives based on regular performance reviews or based on years of service.

Some new business owners have friends and family volunteer to help them out as they're getting things up and running. Depending on your friends and family, this could either be a blessing or a curse. As long as you are able to work well with the people you know, this could be a fine plan, at least for the short term. Keep roles and expectations well-defined, and make sure these volunteers are aware that you are still the boss, and things should work out at least until you've got a full staff helping you out.

Now it comes to actually finding people to apply for your staff positions! There are many ways to do this, and a lot of the process is dependent on your community. You may wish to put out ads on local Facebook groups, letting the area know you are hiring. You'll definitely want to announce job openings on your own social media and website. If you are in a larger city, you may look to post your job openings on sites like Craigslist, or even job sites like Indeed. If you're in a smaller community, you may be able to hang a few signs in strategic locations and get plenty of traffic.

When advertising your job opening, make sure you are as specific as possible about both the duties and the qualifications the ideal candidate will possess. You won't need to list absolutely every detail, for example, "daily cleaning of service area, seating area, and restrooms" should be sufficient for that particular job duty. At the same time, "making coffee" is a very vague representation of all the nuances of preparing drip coffee, pulling espresso shots, and steaming or blending. Make sure that the employees who will need to speak to customers are aware of that particular duty. It is also extremely important to note any physical qualifications at this time, such as "ability to stand for entire shift" or "ability to lift up to fifty pounds." This circles back into the ADA compliance piece as well as labor laws, so make sure prospective employees are aware before they apply if parts of their job may be physically demanding.

We recommend having every person interested in working at your coffee shop fill out an employment application. This document doesn't have to be too terribly in-depth, but will allow you to have a record of the name and general experience of every person who would like to work at your shop. This is great to have on hand any time you need to do some hiring—you can look back on these applications to start. A sample application might include:

- Full name
- Contact info (email and phone number)
- Days available
- Employment history
- References
- Related skills or experience

You may also ask for a brief cover letter or a short explanation of why they are interested in working at your coffee shop, to ensure they are actually interested in following through with the process, and not simply applying because it seemed like a good idea at the time.

You'll also need to make prospective employees aware of any pre-hire background checks, drug tests, and ServSafe certification that they'll need prior to employment. Employees must be informed of and agree to background checks if you choose to have them done. Many employers choose to make employees aware of this process before even conducting interviews. There are legal ramifications of all of these pre-employment requirements, so be sure to study up on your local requirements.

Also, bear in mind why you are doing these tests, and apply the same logic to all employees. The goal is to ensure the employees have been fully honest with you on their applications, and that you can feel at ease about having them handle your money, work face-to-face with your customers, and properly use any equipment you have that may be dangerous. This is not a witch hunt, and you may have to have a few awkward conversations with prospective employees before deciding to hire them. Above all, you want to hire good workers who will get the job done right every single day. This skill often exists beyond any past legal transgressions or a comprehensive education, so be fair and reasonable when evaluating background checks and the like.

This brings up the next thing to keep in mind: What skill set do you want your employees to have? Will you require previous coffee shop experience, or will restaurant experience suffice? If they are extremely skilled in customer service, will you take a chance in training them on how to work in a coffee shop? It's highly unlikely that you will find a full staff that knows every skill you need them to know when they walk through your doors, so decide what you are willing to train, and what skills are an absolute must-have at the offset.

Next, consider what questions you'll ask in your interviews. Remember, there are certain things you legally cannot discuss, so be careful of those topics. Your goal in an interview is to get a feel of the individual's personality, their skills, their comfort in learning new skills, and their willingness to be a team player. You might also want to test their familiarity with a few popular coffee beverages that you'll be selling. Sample questions might include:

- Why do you want to work here?
- How would you react if a customer became angry due to an incorrect order?
- What is your greatest strength? Weakness?
- What are some of the things you look forward to learning in this job?
- What experience makes you feel confident about working here?
- What is the difference between a cappuccino and a latte?

Much as you would not want to be interviewed when you are unprepared, people do not want to be interviewed by someone who is not prepared to conduct the interview. Make sure you have a clear set of questions to ask and take notes as the interview subject speaks. Again, you may not wish to hire this person now, but their information may be relevant at a later date for a future position. Schedule plenty of time in your day to conduct each interview and set aside a quiet place where you will not be interrupted during the interview. Take the time to give them a tour of the space and discuss expectations during the initial interview. While you don't have to give away the recipe to your secret mocha syrup, you will want each candidate to understand their duties and what is expected of them before they sign the employment agreement.

Do not be in such a rush to hire that you ignore red flags. This can be anything from lack of reliable transportation to work, to absolutely no coffee knowledge, to showing up to the interview in inappropriate clothing. While discrimination is strictly illegal, knowing when someone is not a good fit for your coffee shop based on their skills, capabilities, or hygiene is an important part of making good hiring decisions.

At the end of the day, only you will be able to make the call as to which candidates are best for your coffee shop, and what duties you'd like them to fulfill. As you go through the hiring process, make sure you are hiring individuals who can fit into a variety of shifts in your schedule, and who knows or can be trained on a variety of duties. This will ensure you've got enough staff and enough talent to lift your coffee shop into success!

Learning All There is to Know

Eventually, if all goes well and your staff expands according to your vision and plan, someone else will be doing the training. But before your coffee shop opens for its very first day of business, only one person knows how you want things done: YOU!

All businesses should have an Employee Handbook, no matter how basic. This will include things like policies and procedures which will answer all questions, from "what if I can't make my shift" to "how do I request a day off?" You'll want to address sexual harassment, on-the-job injuries, opening procedures, closing procedures, what to do in an emergency, in the event of a fire, in the event of extreme weather, and more. Establishing expectations is the basis of training.

You'll also want a Training Handbook. This will include things like instructions for using all of the equipment, recipes for drinks, instructions for assembling and plating food, as well as the frequency and procedure for cleaning, and more.

The idea of having both the Employee Handbook and the Training Handbook is that you are establishing without a doubt what expectations, duties, roles, and responsibilities belong to whom. In the event of an accident, injury, or incident, you do not want to be caught with any ambiguity or loose ends that could result in a lawsuit or other legal action. Again, this is an area where you may wish to consult with a Human Resources expert or lawyer to make sure you haven't left anything to chance.

You may prefer to schedule one-on-one training with your new staff members, or you may wish to get them together as a group. There are advantages to each, of course, and since you may conduct more than one training session, you might choose to have both types of training sessions. Walk employees through the process of making a drink to your specifications. Let them enter orders on the new Point Of Sale system, or POS. Make up mock orders so they can test each other on their knowledge and the process. Make sure they have a firm grasp of their duties and are confident that they know where they can find information and answers. You may wish to have copies of the handbooks available in the service areas, especially just after you've opened. After all, this is new to everyone. Make it as easy as possible for employees to find the answers and arm them with the information they need to be competent and confident in their jobs.

Walk through the menu. Make sure ingredient lists and recipes are posted where your staff members can easily access them. Make sure these notes are laminated and well bound so they don't wander off or get stained beyond recognition. While it may take a few days for your staff to know the menu by heart, they should be able to guide customers through understanding the difference between item X and item Y on the very first day, even if they have to look it up.

Lastly, consider your employment terms. Most businesses have a training period or probation period, during which time a new staff member is expected to learn everything they need to know—or how and where to find the answer to an obscure question. How long will your probation period be? What is the incentive to completing the probationary period? Will the employees get a boost in salary? An employee discount? Small incentives are helpful in giving employees a clear goal for performing well during the probationary period and beyond.

Be Demanding

You are also in charge of determining what kind of boss you're going to be. Are you going to be hands-on, pitching in when your staff gets overwhelmed? Are you going to be strictly a long-distance boss, in your off-site office until someone calls? Are you going to be intensely "in the trenches" with your employees at first, until everyone has a feel for how the shop is going to run? While everyone has a different management style, as the owner of a business you'll need to set roles, responsibilities, and limitations for yourself, as well.

What will be your discipline style? Many businesses use a "verbal warning, written warning, probation, termination" progression, in which each transgression is addressed with increasingly serious consequences. Then again, what if the error was completely unintentional? How will you mediate disagreements between employees? What sort of actions will lead to disciplinary action, versus a basic re-training conversation? All of this information will need to be in the Employee Handbook, but as the owner of the establishment, it is up to you to enforce all of these policies equally and fairly.

What day-to-day expectations do you have for your staff? Perhaps you expect them to show up ten minutes before their shift, dressed in uniform, and ready to clock in for the day. Who pays for the uniform? Who cleans the uniform? Do they wear name tags? What happens if they lose their name tags? Depending on the materials involved, it might be costly to replace a name tag.

Performance reviews are another place where you will need to practice being demanding. Coaching and feedback should not demean a worker or make them feel like they are incompetent; rather, they should feel like they are being empowered with the information that will take them to the next level in their personal success. Decide when you are going to have performance reviews and stick to that schedule. You may wish to start at the conclusion of the probationary period, each quarter, or annually. Make sure you hold all employees to the same regularity of reviews and hold each employee equally accountable for both their own and the overall business's success.

Furthermore, do not wait for a performance review to discuss concerns or give praise you may have for your staff. Especially in the case of concerns, the actions of your staff may have a negative impact on the overall success of your coffee shop. If another staff member reports questionable actions, or you observe it yourself, investigate and discuss it with that employee in a neutral manner. Remember: miscommunication and misunderstandings are very real things. The only way to resolve these errors is to discuss them calmly in an environment of education, not accusation.

These may seem like micromanaging-level details, but they are truly required considerations when managing staff. There are many, many things to keep in mind as an employer. Many of your actions can and will have legal ramifications. They'll also have personal repercussions. The first time you have to terminate an employee, it will feel awful for everyone involved. Make sure that you are armed with a plan that meets all of the state and federal legal regulations, and be prepared for every eventuality. You might feel oddly paranoid and out of your element, so feel free to seek professional employment guidance, but rest assured that knowing how to handle a situation will make it easier to follow through in the event that you really need to do so.

Of course, you want to be kind and fair, but just like any setting, there will be rules that must be followed, or consequences will ensue. You will best serve the success of your company if you are fair, yet demanding. Respectful, yet unwavering. Empathetic, but not pathetic. As the owner of this coffee shop, you are the leader. You should both command and deserve respect.

Step 8: Planning for the Big Day

At this point, your vision has become a reality. You've enacted a plan from square one. You've got a perfect, well-groomed space, from which you're going to sell your carefully curated collection of coffee and more. The scene is set, the beans are ground, and the staff is eager to serve their first customer. This is the moment you've been waiting for!

Setting the Stage

There's one last thing you need to do before you let customers in: set the menu and the prices. You'll want to make sure the menu is prominently displayed—no one likes to guess at what you serve and how much it costs.

When it comes to creating a menu, make sure it is legible in every way. Make sure the spelling and punctuation are correct. Make sure the wording is large and clear. Make sure any interesting ingredients or notes are available for customers to consider. Some cafes have large menus posted overhead for customers to read, and small handheld or paper menus where they can read more about flavors and aroma notes. Customers will need to be aware of what they should expect when they take that first sip, so these notes will help set those expectations.

Depending on your anticipated clientele, you may want to avoid being too creative with the naming of your beverages as well. Using the banana-and-chocolate example from earlier, consider whether your customers will be comfortable ordering a "Bananafanana-fo-foffee," or if something like "Mocha Banana Royale" both accurately describes the drink while being accessible to your audience. Make sure drink names actually relate to the drink, as well. Being too creative can lead to more questions, and if you're looking to have a rush of customers seeking that morning hit of caffeine, they'll be less likely to want to ask questions and do research. They just want a delicious drink in their hands before they face another busy day.

Pricing... is a delicate matter, to say the least. The price of coffee varies so widely that the coffee shop model is often used in business classes. A lot of factors will dictate your pricing, especially the going rate of coffee in your area. Try to stay in the same range as your direct competitors, as this will encourage people that your product is just as much of a value as other cafes in the area. All that said, though, your pricing should include:

- Cost of coffee
- Cost of labor
- Cost of takeaway cup and lid
- Cost of any additional ingredients
- Cost of any cream/sugar/etc

All of these costs can be calculated from the business accounts you've been tracking diligently through this entire process. Calculating the cost of supplies will be the easiest part since this likely does not waiver. A cup of house blend will require a certain portion of a bag of beans. If you pay $10 for a bag of beans, and a cup of house blend requires 1/100th of a bag of beans, then your cost for that cup of coffee is 10 cents. To determine labor, consider how long it takes to actually prepare and serve that drink, compared to the worker's hourly salary.

Then, on top of this, determine what you want your profit margin to be. You can certainly visit the accountant again if this part is confusing. Altogether, the profit margin should be enough to pay for all of your supplies, ingredients, staff, rent/mortgage, loan, and a bit for yourself. The profit margin may not be the same for every customer and every drink. For example, a customer who has a drink "for here," will not need the takeaway cup and lid. A customer who drinks their coffee plain will not incur the costs for cream and sugar. You won't charge them differently, however. That would be far too complicated at the outset. Instead, when you're calculating profit margin, you'll expect that a portion of customers will make you a little less profit than others.

At this point, you may feel completely confused by the entire game and wish to rush through this process. Do not give in to this temptation. Simply stay calm and do the math … or pay your accountant to do so.

The Final Walkthrough

Before you even consider opening, make sure you have scheduled all of your final requirements. Make sure all of your deliveries have been scheduled appropriately so that they don't overlap, but that all of your supplies and products arrive on time. You'll need time to get all of the storage containers sanitized and ready to use. You'll need to make sure any refrigeration has been inspected and cleared for use. Your local ordinances may require a final walkthrough of the building before issuing your building and business permits. You'll need time to make sure uniforms are cleaned and pressed, furniture assembled and cleaned, artwork hung, and music playlists sorted.

There should be one final, peaceful moment in between all the last-minute melee where you have the ability to walk through one final time before opening. Take full advantage of this moment. For the past several months, you have been engulfed in your coffee shop from the standpoint of an owner. Any time you've looked at the setting, you've looked at it with the careful gaze of someone who needs to make sure everything is perfect and in the most correct spot.

Now, take the time to look at it as a connoisseur. Sit in a chair and think of how a customer will feel at your cafe. This is the final moment for last-minute adjustments, so let everything soak in. Is the lighting at the right level of brightness? Is the music too loud or too soft? When the machinery is working, is it obnoxiously loud? Is the smell of coffee too strong, or just right? This is your last chance to make modifications to anything, from acoustics to the seating layout. Use this time wisely to ensure everything meets that original vision and plan.

The next few sections will include some tips for both a soft opening and a Grand Opening. These are included to help guide you through the process. You may choose to go a completely different direction for your coffee shop, based on your experience, comfort, community, and more. That is absolutely fine. If you are looking to celebrate the opening of your new cafe in a big way, or just need some tips for drawing a crowd right off the bat, read on!

Planning Your Grand Opening

Many cafes and restaurant owners like to do a quiet, "soft" opening before their official, public Grand Opening. Having some form of a soft opening allows you to shake out any last-minute wrinkles before the general public is allowed to stop by, so if there's a drink recipe that needs tweaking or any gaps in the service flow amongst staff members, this is a great time to address them.

Sometimes this takes the form of an invite-only event, in which your team is cordially invited to visit your coffee shop for a grand reveal. This could include anyone who has made this dream a reality, including your friends, family, accountant, contractors, designers, landlord or realty agent, lawyer, marketing assistants, your staff's friends and family, investors... the list can go on and on. Having a quiet reveal party like this will be a warm "thank you" for all of the help these folks have provided to you.

You may also wish to casually open the doors before the grand opening and see who wanders in. This form of a soft opening allows you additional training opportunities for staff—they get to actually serve real guests, but everyone understands this is not the full out and formal experience.

Once you choose the date for your Grand Opening, it is set in stone in the eyes of the community, so be absolutely sure you're ready to go. If you're going to put it on your menu, it should be available. The staff should be in uniform, trained, and prepared. The dishes should be spotless and neatly stacked, and that shiny gleam of newness should greet each brand new patron.

If you are anything less than completely ready, do not proceed. Here are some things to check off before you unlock that door to the public:

1. Do you have all the ingredients for all of your drinks and snacks?
2. Do you have a tidy, attractive way to serve them all?
3. Is the POS system working correctly?
4. Do you have change to give guests who pay in cash?
5. Is the staff fully trained on when to serve, clean, assemble, etc?
6. Is everyone in uniform, ready to greet customers warmly?
7. Are all of the fixtures and furnishings installed and ready to be used?
8. Are there any signs of construction (wires, pipes, drywall, sheeting, etc)?
9. Are the restrooms fully stocked and functional?
10. Does the parking lot look attractive and safe?

If you can answer YES to all of these questions, you are ready for your Grand Opening!

What Will Make Your Day Special?

Your first day of business will undoubtedly be very special for you and your staff. After all, you've been working toward this magical moment for as long as you can remember! In order to encourage more people to come out to your Grand Opening, it's a good idea to do something special to celebrate the day.

This, of course, can take many shapes, depending on the focus of your coffee shop and your community. If your vision was around a meeting place for artistic and creative types, maybe you have an exhibition of local artists to coincide with your first official day of business. If you're going with the "gourmet experience" type of coffee shop, perhaps you pull out a very rare and special bean for the big day. You can invite local celebrities, have the local radio station attend … whatever will get the word out in your specific area and draw attention to your fabulous new business in a positive way can be a great way to start off your new venture.

Remember, of course, that there will be hiccups along the way—things likely won't always go as planned. Just like any big event, the weather may not cooperate, something technical will fail, and you'll have to come up with a workaround. Breathe deeply and go with the flow. Short of having to cancel the entire thing, a well-entertained and pleased crowd will also go with the flow and appreciate that you don't have control over everything.

If you are going to plan things like celebrities, musical performances, a ceremony with the mayor, and the like, make sure you plan out the day's schedule well beforehand, with a significant amount of padding in between events. You will not want to be rushed, as you may have minor catastrophes to attend to throughout the course of the day. Have plenty of time for things to flow out, with your new beverages and snacks taking center stage any time there's a break in the action.

It's also a great idea to announce your Grand Opening anywhere possible. Going back to the marketing plans, make sure your Grand Opening celebration is posted on your website. Include a count-down clock, if you wish. People get excited when they're given a specific time frame for an event, so encourage it! Get people hyped on your social media accounts and add your event information to any local event page that will have it. You may have to pay a small fee to have it added to local news event calendars, but a small fee could be recouped in just a few sales, so it will likely be worth it.

Put up signs as you're permitted—at places where the public congregates, along the road, in front of your door. Scream from the mountaintops if you wish—just make sure you do everything to make sure as many people as possible know about your event!

Special Deals for a Special Day

You might have seen businesses that offer a special coupon that's good for Opening Day only. These are the types of flyers you might see on your car windshield or stuffed in a mailbox. There are both good and not-so-good things about special offers on a Grand Opening day. While you are definitely likely to entice customers to come in and use that coupon, you will be selling product at a reduced rate, and you will have to pay for the flyers to be printed. Plus, there's the matter of distributing them in the first place.

Instead, you may wish to offer a very special drink that's ONLY available on Opening Day. Many people find it very hard to resist a limited time offer. You can also serve something special, such as a free piece of "birthday" cake while supplies last. You want to encourage people to fall in love with your product, but you don't want your Grand Opening to drive you further into debt. Free small samples are a good option, as they are often low-cost and low-waste, while demonstrating your amazing product. Also, as the business owner, remember not to get caught up in the excitement and give away the proverbial farm.

Consider, however, having coupons at your register, or handing them out to people in person at your Grand Opening event. This will encourage them to come back a second time, to spend even more money, and become impressed with you all over again. Make sure your social media and web address are prominently displayed, and hint that you'll be making future special offers there. That will encourage people to follow you on social media, which will keep your business name fresh in their minds every time they check their feed.

What Do You Need When You Need a Helper?

This may come as a shock, but you will not be able to run your Grand Opening alone. The coffee grinder will choose this moment to become stuck. The phone will ring off the hook. Someone will need to take care of traffic in the parking lot. Your star barista will suddenly blank on what goes into your signature drink. Something will drop and spill and require immediate cleanup.

You would do well to have your entire staff on hand during the Grand Opening. It will be an incredible learning experience that they can all reference, going forward. They'll be able to help each other out with the learning curve. Just make sure they don't all get in each other's way, so shift out and rotate as necessary.

You may also wish to have a few volunteers for this event. These can be team members, friends and family, or local volunteers who are willing to come out for the day to make sure no one double-parks. Whatever you choose, make sure these individuals are well-informed in their duties, and where to find you in case things get out of hand.

Due to high-traffic concerns, you may also need to alert the local emergency services of your Grand Opening, especially if you're expecting a big crowd. Check your local ordinances, because it would be the ultimate bummer to have your party shut down due to an avoidable violation.

Once your team is assembled, make sure you have time to rehearse everything. Make sure everyone knows where everything is located, and that roles and duties for this special day are carefully defined. The last thing you need is drama between two parties of overzealous volunteers! Doing anything last minute is unavoidable, but make sure the largest moving pieces of the grand opening are addressed long before the first customer pulls into the parking lot.

Be Prepared

Lastly, remember that this is the first day of the rest of your life. Maybe it won't be the raging bash you thought it was going to be. Maybe it snows. Maybe someone trips in the parking lot and injures themselves. Do not go into panic mode.

Have everything rehearsed and ready to go. Extra electrical extension cords. Duct tape for miles. Beans at the ready, and towers of to-go cups. It may feel a bit like you're going into battle, and in a sense, you are. You are conquering this community on behalf of your coffee shop.

Furthermore, be prepared for things to go wrong, as mentioned earlier. Having things like walkie-talkies, or cell phones within reach, will help you and everyone helping you run the event communicate, especially if the setting is noisy or the locations too far apart to shout. Walk through and rehearse how things should go, and make sure everyone is aware of where the phones, extra supplies, first aid kit, and additional stock will be located. Stage everything for success, too. For example, if trash bags are normally kept under the counter in a cabinet, perhaps they can be placed in a cabinet closer to the trash cans for today. Maybe instead of happily being locked away in the office, register tape sits next to the register today, so it can easily be changed in between customers. Plan for super-hyper-efficiency. You only get one chance to make a first impression!

No matter what happens the first day, learn and move on. Any mistakes are hereby considered "learning experiences." Anything that doesn't work out quite right will be assessed and reviewed. Whatever the weak link is, become bolder and better. As we've mentioned several times, building a business starts with a vision and a plan, but it is a continual process to keep that vision and plan fresh and viable and running smoothly.

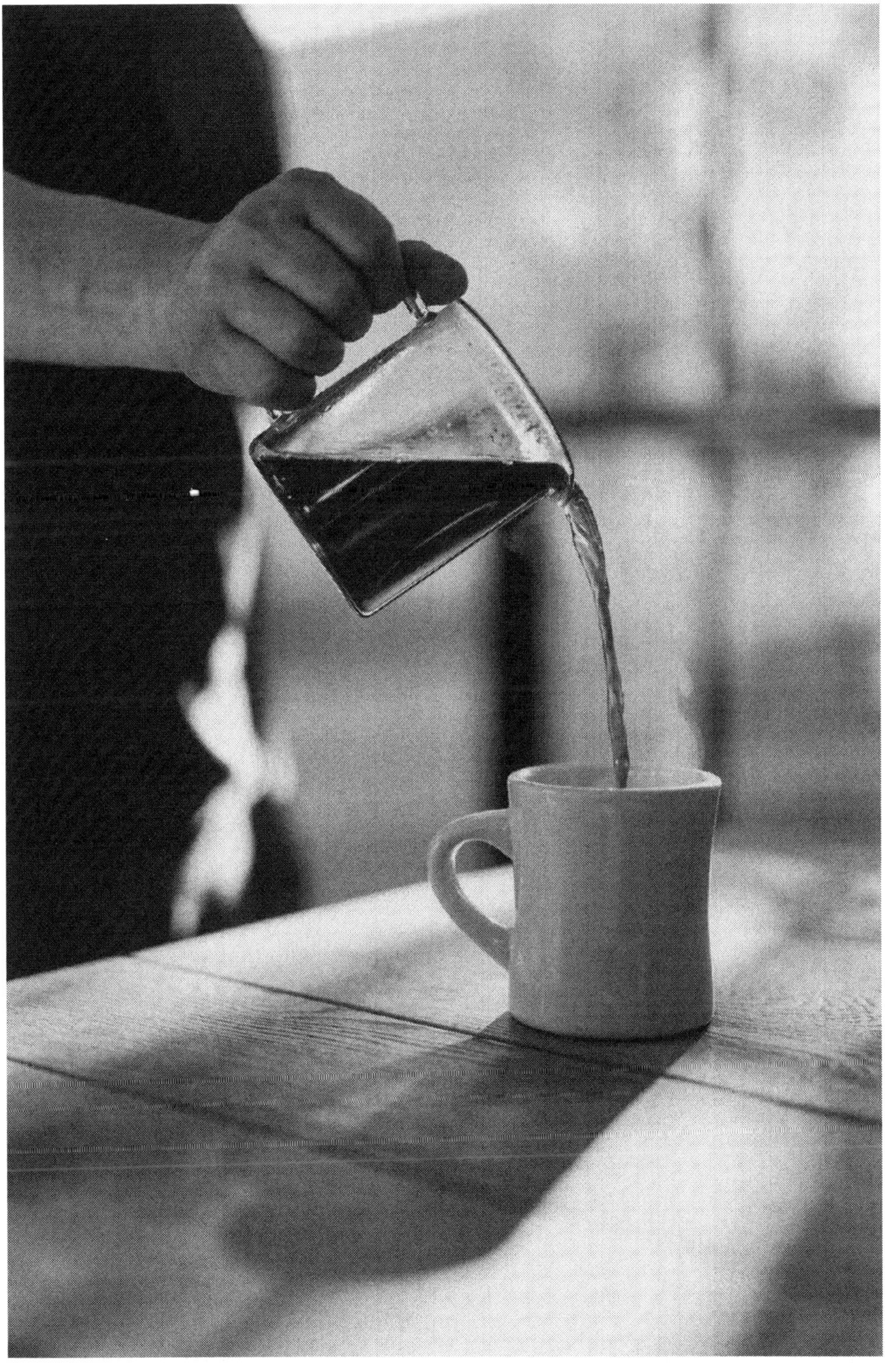

Business as Usual

And just like that, it has finally happened. What started many long months or years ago as a vision and a plan has become a full-fledged coffee shop. Your hard work has paid off. All of those moments of anger, frustration, and sadness, of feeling overwhelmed and under-prepared … all of them have led to the moment when you can reach over your counter, hand a customer their order, and say, "Thank you for stopping at my coffee shop today."

Every day will be a different day. Some days you will panic about customers and money. Some days you will be fully in the weeds, wondering when you'll have time to restock the coffee bar or take out the trash. After a brilliant opening period, you'll start to learn what "normal" business looks like for your cafe. You'll learn the names of the regulars. You know when the rushes come. You'll understand which drinks sell like crazy, and which are terrific flops.

As time goes by, you'll learn more about your business, and become more and more comfortable with the ins and outs of the business decisions. You'll get inventory needs down to a science and the menu down to an art. Don't ever be afraid to make adjustments, but as any keen person in sales and marketing will tell you, don't get rid of your biggest hits.

Perhaps, as the years go by, you'll be interested in expanding your wildly popular brand. Perhaps you'll play it safe and stay with the tried-and-true method that is serving you well today. You may wish to try out new ideas, new recipes, new events, but remember, the success you are experiencing now is based on what you are doing now. Anything that doesn't work now will continue to not work well unless it is adjusted.

Coaching and feedback are not only useful for your staff, but for you, as well. Stay connected to your customers. Learn what they love and don't love about your shop. Respond to their needs—don't ignore complaints and concerns. Encourage communication from your customers, because that will help you know what they enjoy about your shop. Remember, you are essentially running this business for them. Without customers, there are no sales, and with no sales, there's no cafe!

Every day that you open the doors for business, let yourself feel fulfilled by the vision and plan that started this whole thing. Let yourself feel pride for a job well done, and for making it through one of the most intense processes of your life. Think back on how you navigated the budget. What issues you encountered when finding the location and preparing it. The trials and tribulations that went into choosing your menu. We encourage you to keep all of your notes from the process. Those rejected recipes might come through as a new favorite someday! Furthermore, those small pieces of the dream that didn't make it into your coffee shop's first iteration may someday be incorporated into a remodel or refresh. Don't put everything to bed—instead, collect and relish your memories. These are the daydreams that came true.

Conclusion

We hope you have enjoyed this journey through the basic process of opening your own coffee shop. Whether you're staring at a cup of hot joe right now, thinking how ready you are to start the process, or if you're trying to decide if that's the caffeine jitters or a serious case of nerves, we hope that the information presented here gives you a sense of what you'll need to keep in mind when opening your flagship cafe.

Please bear in mind that this is to be considered as a general guide for opening your own coffee shop. As we stated in the beginning, it was written with the standards of practice for the United States in mind. Each state has tons of different requirements and regulations on all of the aspects of running a business; in fact, there are so many, we could write a book for each state. Therefore, we tried to keep things simple and streamlined, but you will absolutely need to check with the state regulations before setting up your own business. We have included some helpful links in the index to get you started on the research path, but remember, regulations change quickly, so you may wish to consult with a professional to ensure everything you're doing and all of your practices are legal, correct, and accurate.

As we've stated several times in this book, there are times in which it is best to get a professional's advice. Leaving things to chance is never recommended. Asking for help is never a bad thing. While this book is intended to set you on a solid path of considerations and options when opening your own coffee shop, there's no way we can anticipate every situation you may encounter on your own path. In fact, there may be times the professionals on your team even say, "Wow, we did not see that coming!"

We encourage you to take a look at some of the links in the index for further guidance. We hope that you'll be filled with inspiration and motivation to consider research that is more personalized to your very own coffee shop. None of the links we have included are intended to be endorsements, but rather examples of some of the resources that are out there.

This book required significant research, and the words of wisdom of many experts in many different fields have been incorporated into each chapter. As you proceed down the path of opening your own cafe, consider building your own team of mentors. Interview people in the local food scene. Get a feel for what works for them and what doesn't. Join professional groups—both in person and on social media—now. Start obsessively visiting coffee shops everywhere you go. Make notes about how things vary in your neighborhood from spots in other towns, cities, states, and so on. This is going to be your hard-earned dream come true, so gather your allies and keep yourself informed!

Congratulations on your choice to pursue your own business. You deserve plenty of praise for your dedication to your vision and your plan. We hope your business thrives and flourishes, and that you someday are able to pass your own words of wisdom down to the next generation of local entrepreneurs!

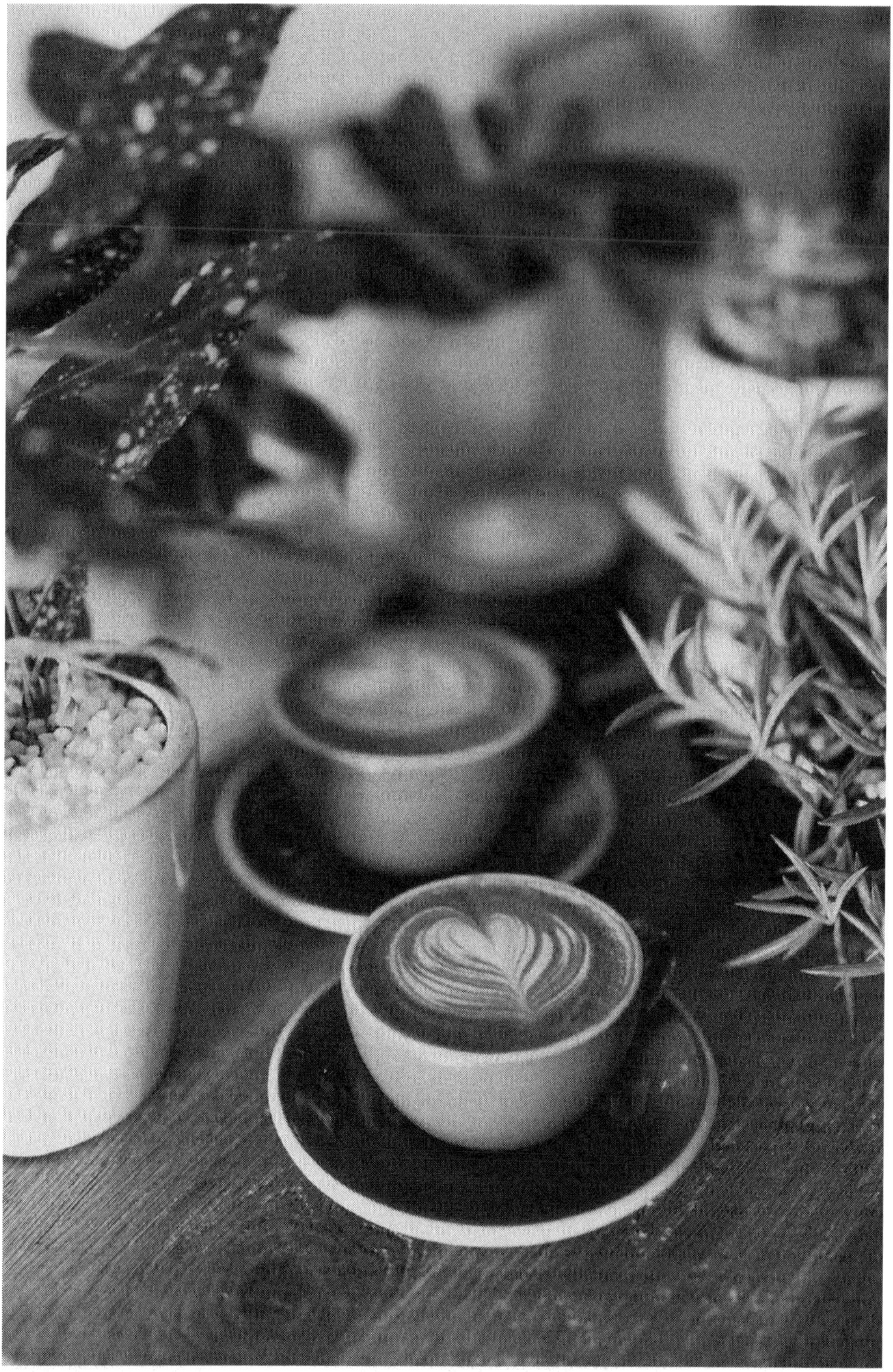

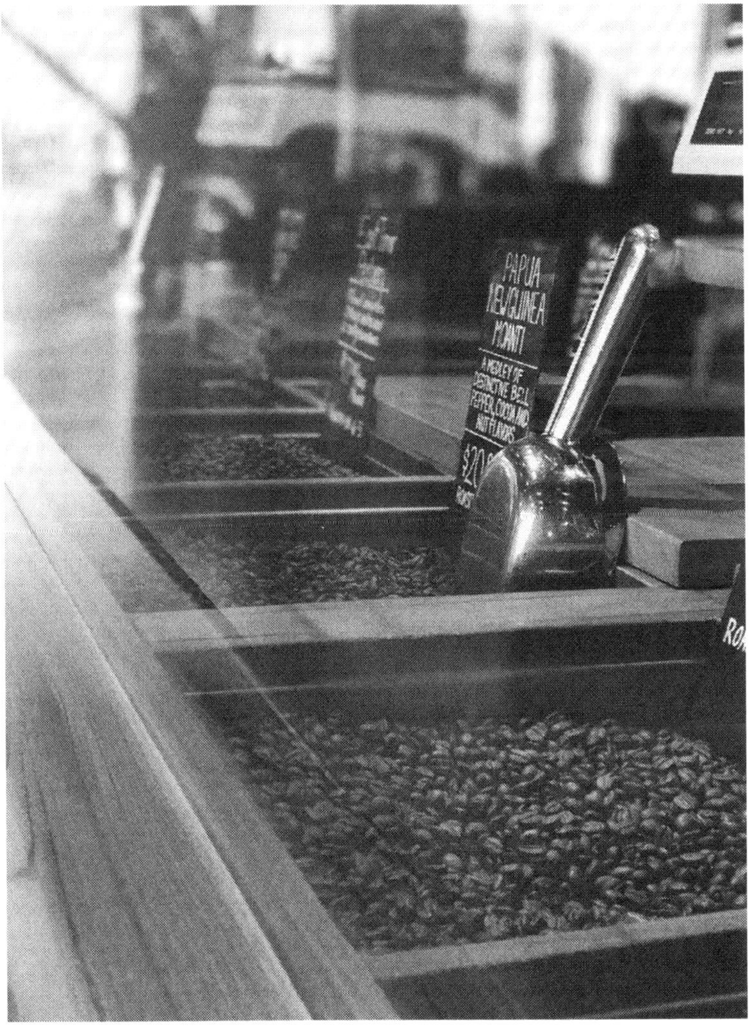
PAPUA
NEW GUINEA

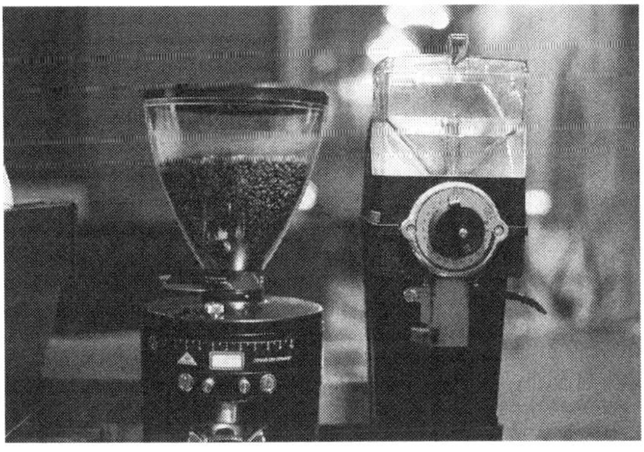

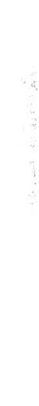

Index

As noted throughout the text, here are a few helpful links we've collected to inspire you. These are grouped by topic, so you can choose the sections and areas that might best help you at each stage in the process.

Legal Considerations

The following links will guide you to Federal and State websites that outline a variety of health, safety, employment, and discrimination requirements. It is highly recommended that you give each of these a thorough read before even starting the process of creating a business plan. This list is not all-inclusive; however, you will be led through a variety of points and considerations when gauging all of the legal requirements that govern your location.

OSHA: Occupational Health and Safety Administration. This agency exists within the United States Department of Labor and works to ensure proper and safe working conditions for all.
https://www.osha.gov/SLTC/restaurant/standards.html
https://www.osha.gov/SLTC/foodbornedisease/standards.html)

FDA: The Food and Drug Administration is a federal agency within the United States Department of Health and Human Services, protecting the health of the public with regulations that ensure the safety of food and food supplies.
https://www.fda.gov/food/fda-food-code/state-retail-and-food-service-codes-and-regulations-state

ADA: The Americans With Disabilities Act is a civil rights law that prohibits any kind of discrimination based on disability. ADA Compliance is granted by adhering to a number of regulations that cover everything from public accommodations to employment.
 https://www.ada.gov/smbustxt.htm

ServSafe: a program administered by the National Restaurant Association that provides sanitation certification that is required for many in the food industry.
https://www.servsafe.com/ServSafe-Food-Handler/Buy-Handler-Products?gclid=CjoKC-Qjw6eTtBRDdARIsANZWjYa1BP3ynkJLinuDteqwvhTw6t4cv-0giwD_nCjAZQGhgKpBZRQ-6J2kaAhDeEALw_wcB

State Health Departments: This list helps you locate your state health department for information about requirements that are specific to your state.
https://healthfinder.gov/FindServices/SearchContext.aspx?topic=820&show=1

US Department of Labor: These links will help you discover the Federal laws and regulations surrounding safely and legally hiring and maintaining employment for your new staff.
https://www.dol.gov/general/aboutdol/majorlaws, https://www.usa.gov/labor-laws, https://www.dol.gov/general/location

EEOC: The United States Equal Employment Opportunity Commission has also issued a series of laws and regulations, which can help you avoid unintentional discrimination.
https://www.eeoc.gov/laws/practices/

IRS: Internal Revenue Service, which handles employment taxes and all of the forms required when hiring a new employee.
https://www.irs.gov/businesses/small-businesses-self-employed/hiring-employees

Employment Lawyer: This resource can help you avoid and remove yourself legally from possible predicaments you may encounter when setting up your employees and practices.
http://www.myemploymentlawyer.com/

Financial Links

In Step 2, we mention a few sources for funding and gathering investors. The following sites were mentioned in that chapter, so we have linked them here. You may also wish to talk to agents and specialists at local banks, credit unions, and other financial institutions. Interest rates and loan requirements will vary from location to location, so shopping around will help you gauge the best option for you and your budget.

Small Business Association: Support and connections for entrepreneurs wading into the waters of starting a small business.
https://www.sba.gov/

Swift Capital: Another resource specializing in connecting small business owners with funding.
https://www.swiftcapital.com/

Prosper, TrustLeaf, OnDeck, and Lending Club: Connections to investors and lenders for your area, your business, and your ideas.

www.prosper.com

https://www.facebook.com/trustleaf/

www.ondeck.com

www.lendingclub.com

National Business Incubation Association: A global network of incubators, entrepreneurs, accelerators, and mentors for new business owners.

https://inbia.org/

Angel Networks: Groups of investors and entrepreneurs established with the sole goal of helping up-and-coming business owners with financial and practical support.

https://www.angelcapitalassociation.org/

https://www.angelinvestmentnetwork.us/

Crowdfunding: Websites that allow interested, independent parties to make donations to your cause. Be sure to read their rules and requirements before setting up your account!

www.kickstarter.com

www.ourcrowd.com

www.indiegogo.com

Technology

We mentioned a few ways in which technology can aid you in staying organized. We also mentioned sites that can help you with marketing, such as creating a logo and a webpage.

Floor plan creation and simulation: These programs can help you enter measurements to create your perfect floor plan, allowing you to accurately fit all of the furnishings and fixtures in all the right spots.

https://floorplancreator.net/

https://www.smartdraw.com/floor-plan/floor-plan-designer.htm

https://floorplanner.com/

Logo Creation: These sites can help you dream up your idea logo, either for a small fee, or completely free!

https://www.wix.com/logo/maker

https://placeit.net/logo-maker
https://www.freelogodesign.org/

Website: We mentioned WordPress as a possible website tool. Here's a link to learn more about their services.
https://wordpress.com/

Supply Chain

Please note that not all of these suppliers will contract with every location or every type of business. These links are intended as a launchpad for reviewing possibilities in your area and for your specific cafe. Additionally, many of these suppliers offer a variety of services that go beyond their listing in the directory below.

Uniforms, Linens, Sanitation: These vendors offer a variety of services that help keep your cafe clean and up to code. Some offer a very wide variety of services, including inventory and more, so take a look at all each one has to offer.
https://www.cintas.com/facilityservices/
https://www.sysco.com/
https://www.therdstore.com/

Equipment Specific to Coffee Shops and Cafes: For your espresso machines, grinders, drip brew, and more, it's best to start with experts. These companies market specifically to coffee shop owners and those who sell large quantities of professional-grade coffee.
https://www.webstaurantstore.com/restaurant-equipment.html   https://www.coffeeam.com/wholesale-1/cafe-equipment-packages.html   https://www.voltagerestaurantsupply.com/

Coffee Beans and Supplies: Exotic, gourmet, delicious, and more. These vendors specialize in coffee beans for coffee shops. When purchasing your beans, make sure you're not settling for anything you wouldn't like to be sold yourself!
https://www.kaldi.com/wholesale-coffee   https://www.coffeeam.com/wholesale-1/wholesale-coffee.html
https://www.specialtyjava.com/wholesale.htm

Food, Food Supplies, Ingredients: These vendors can set you up with regular deliveries of the food, food supplies, and ingredients that will keep you in business. Many of these suppliers also have physical storefronts you can visit, to get a feel for their product and quality. Check out their websites for more information.

https://www.sysco.com/

https://www.foodservicedirect.com/

https://www.foodsupply.com/

https://www.gfs.com/en-us

www.usfoods.com

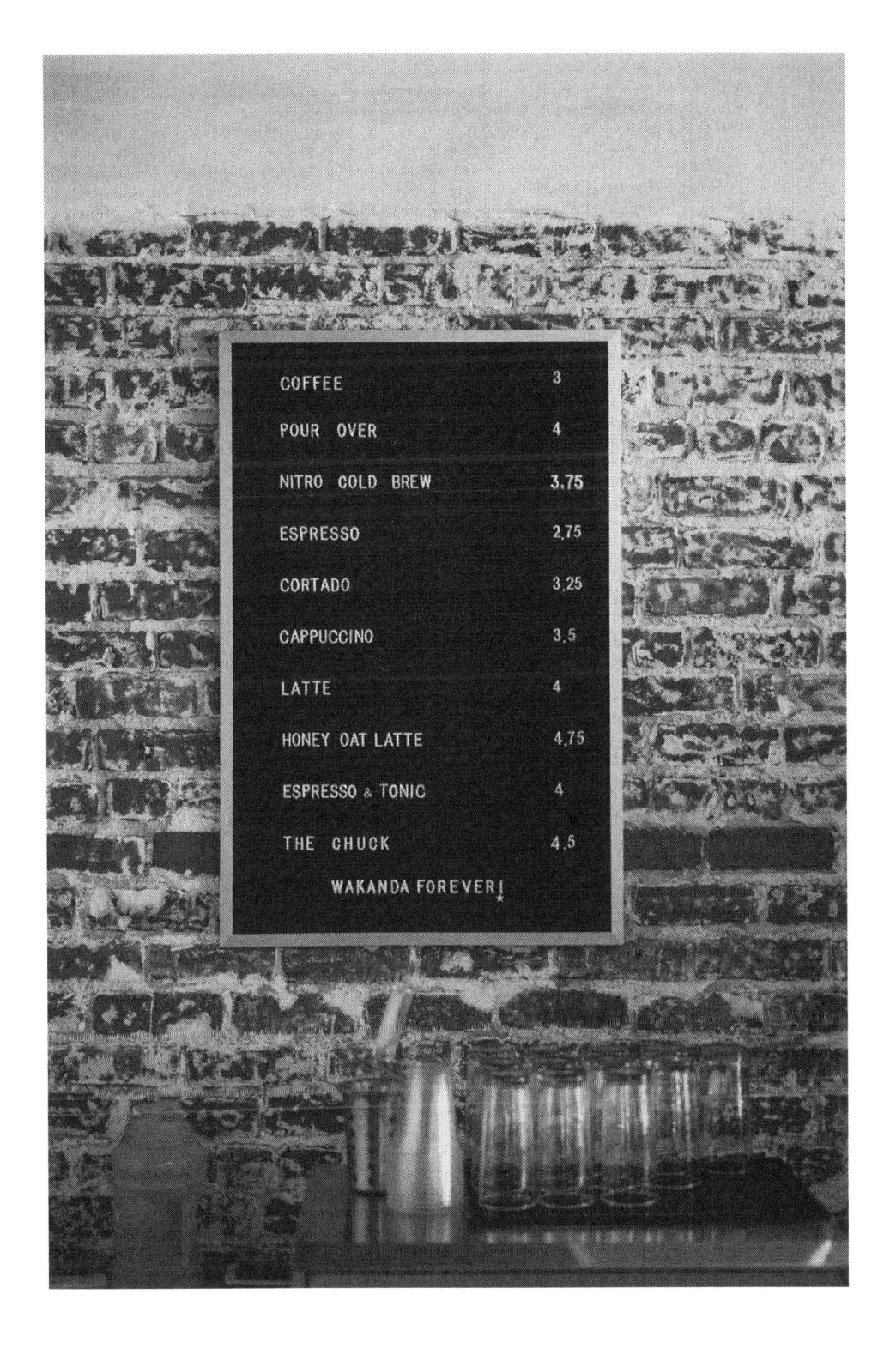

COFFEE	3
POUR OVER	4
NITRO COLD BREW	3,75
ESPRESSO	2,75
CORTADO	3,25
CAPPUCCINO	3,5
LATTE	4
HONEY OAT LATTE	4,75
ESPRESSO & TONIC	4
THE CHUCK	4,5

WAKANDA FOREVER!

Reviews

Reviews and feedback help improve this book and the author. If you enjoy this book, we would greatly appreciate it if you could take a few moments to share your opinion and post a review on Amazon.

also by Stella Perry

Brewing and More. How to Enjoy Coffee Beyond Your Morning Routine

mybook.to/RoastingCoffee

© 2019

Printed in Poland
by Amazon Fulfillment
Poland Sp. z o.o., Wrocław